RIGGED

HOW NETWORKS OF POWERFUL MATES RIP OFF EVERYDAY AUSTRALIANS

CAMERON K. MURRAY & PAUL FRIJTERS

ALLEN&UNWIN
SYDNEY • MELBOURNE • AUCKLAND • LONDON

This edition published in 2022

First published as *Game of Mates* by Cameron K. Murray & Paul Frijters in 2017

Allen & Unwin
83 Alexander Street
Crows Nest NSW 2065
Australia
Phone: (61 2) 8425 0100
Email: info@allenandunwin.com
Web: www.allenandunwin.com

We acknowledge all First Nations lands on which we work.

 A catalogue record for this book is available from the National Library of Australia

ISBN 978 1 76106 766 2

Illustrations by Carissa Harris
Set in 11.5/18 pt Sabon LT Pro by Midland Typesetters, Australia
Printed in Australia by Pegasus Media & Logistics

10 9 8 7 6 5 4 3 2

To our children and their children

Contents

Preface

Rigged was first published as *Game of Mates* in 2017. It was an amateur booklet, printed on demand from who-knows-where. We did all the marketing ourselves, meaning a garage stacked with boxes to be sent to bookstores and events. The many spelling mistakes were such an embarrassment that we felt forced within weeks to put out a slightly adjusted version, though we didn't really tell anyone. We still have some of the originals in boxes. We give them out to friends of the forgiving type.

While the production of the book was amateur, the content was not. The ideas in it had been brewing since 2010 when both authors independently discovered the true depths of the corruption that had taken hold of Queensland and Australia. Cameron was working in a regulatory office, witnessing one scandal after another, with the corrupt usually in charge and getting away with it. Paul was then at the Queensland University of Technology, or as he secretly thought of it 'The Banana Republic of

Queensland'. It was the time when the Mayor of Brisbane gave the company of his wife contracts worth millions, when the politicians appointed someone they could trust as the head of the Supreme Court, and when vice-chancellors wrote bogus reports to support the decision of the politicians to replace the head of the anti-corruption body with an insider to the property market corruption scams. At the national level, the Gillard government had just given billions of dollars' worth of concessions to a mining industry that was largely owned by foreigners and that had run a very successful anti-government campaign, allowing them to dictate terms to the government. The foxes were hence taking over the chicken coops left, right and centre, not even bothering to hide the blood on their teeth. The brazen nature of the corruption was matched only by the general apathy of the population that by and large had their heads firmly stuck in the sand, angry at every attempt to make them see what was going on.

Both of us strongly felt the situation was wrong and had to be documented and analysed dispassionately. We set up several research projects, spent a lot of time thinking about how it all fitted together, and eventually decided that our findings needed to be put into an easy-read format in which highly complex matters were boiled down to their essentials. This led to us telling the story in *Game of Mates* of James, the connected insider, and our everyday Australian who is fleeced by the Game James plays, who we then called Bruce but now call Sam. We did of course also write 'proper' research papers for high-level academic journals (and got them published), but the point of that was to have street-cred and technical feedback. Academic papers were a step along the road, not the finish line.

The credit for this updated version should go to the team at Allen & Unwin, and particularly Richard Walsh. Richard liked the original book and reached out to us about whether we would be willing to write an update and extension to the first edition. He and his team persisted, despite some reluctance on our part to again engage with the dark side of Australia, telling us the effort was needed. Good on 'em. So thanks to the entire Allen & Unwin team: Elizabeth Weiss, Tom Bailey-Smith, Susan Keogh, and our illustrator, Carissa Harris.

In the intervening five years, corruption and political favouritism only became worse in Australia. We joked that *Game of Mates* was not a 'how to' guide, but we suspect that many purchasers gave the book to their sons and daughters with the message 'Read this. We're James. This book tells you what we do and how we do it.' Rather like how the film *The Godfather* is particularly popular among Mafiosi who started to behave like the characters in those films, we suspect that we too have created a mould for how the corrupt in Australia conduct themselves. It was not the intention, but perhaps inevitable. James always does the early running. Yet Sam's move is ultimately more decisive.

Our wish with *Rigged* is the same as with *Game of Mates*; to simply explain how politics in Australia truly works and thus the degree to which the majority is unnecessarily short-changed and belittled. We lay out how it is done, our best estimates for how much it matters and our best suggestions for how the situation can be remedied. Our hope is that a broader movement in Australia emerges oriented towards a renewal of the Aussie spirit, and that that movement will find some value in this book.

In our estimation, the medium-run future of Australia looks bleak. The international reputation of the country got a knock during the Covid years (2020–2022) as the country closed its borders and became seen by others as a nation bereft of empathy towards anyone who would not toe the line. The school disruptions, disruptions to the health system, forced social distancing and forced business closures furthermore created huge misery and long-lasting damage to the production and skill-base of the country. The government could only keep a lid on the underlying impoverishment that the Covid policies led to by printing enormous amounts of money, distributed disproportionately to the wealthiest.

We expect the next five years or so to see a lot of political unrest as the impoverishment and division becomes clear and the fight over the nation's wealth becomes bitter. That might evolve into something positive, like a strong reform movement that wants to renew the Aussie spirit. Or it might evolve into something very ugly indeed, like a fascist movement that blames the problems on some defenceless section of society and then tries to socially, or perhaps even physically, eliminate them. We hope for the best.

Yet in the longer run, we think the outlook of Australia is still fantastic. It has a socially cohesive population, low crime rates, high basic health, lots of natural resources, an underlying warm egalitarian culture and is in an area of the world that is still on an historical upwards trajectory. Once Australians refocus on being productive and fair, rather than hoping for crumbs off the table, we see no reason for Australia not to prosper. We do not know exactly when the reform wave will happen that Australia needs to have to get to that brighter future, but we are confident it will happen and that there are plenty of good ideas that can then be implemented. Sam, you'll be right once again, but only after some hard yakka.

1
A Loathsome Tale

Rigged is the story of how Australia became one of the most unequal societies in the Western world, while a generation ago it was one of the most equal.[1] It is the story of how groups of Mates have rigged our corporate and political sectors, and managed to rob us, the Australian majority, of over half our wealth.

To understand how the Game of Mates is played and to disrupt it, we must see Australia through the eyes of our villain, whom we call James. In reality, the Game of Mates is played by well-connected individuals called Eddie, Peter, Gladys and so forth. Only rarely are they truly named James, and we of course do not want to offend any James out there who is not a villain.

This book is about how the Jameses of this country play their Game of Mates. It is about how much their Game costs you, and what we can do to stop them.

Opposing our villain is our champion Aussie, whom we call Sam. Sam represents the men and women who are complete outsiders and never benefit from the Game of Mates. In each chapter, we show how much James's Game ends up costing Sam, bleeding Sam and Sam's family not only of their current wealth, but tying them to future obligations to pay James for the privilege of taking part in society.

Our characters help to tell a story that is difficult to see from the perspective of any individual. The reality of the Game of Mates in practice is far less tantalising than the fantasy worlds of political intrigue we see on screen. Brilliant as these stories are, the reality of Australia's insidious political games is far more ordinary—Sam bleeds economically, rather than from the neck. Our villain James swings no sword. He does not ambush Sam in physical attacks. He instead swings his power in the halls of parliament, in the media and in the complex bureaucracies of government and large corporate enterprises. His ambush is a raid on Sam's wealth that happens on the sly in mundane offices across our cities, but that nevertheless takes a cut of the country's economic wealth to which he was never entitled. Instead of victory parades, James hosts industry awards nights to glowing media coverage.

The not-so-bloody reality is that James has been in the ascendancy in Australia for at least the last twenty years. He now robs you of a hefty part of your superannuation. He dodges taxes so you pay more. You pay higher interest rates on your mortgage, higher transport costs and higher medical costs, because James and his Mates take a cut.

Our research leads us to believe that James is stealing roughly half of the real wealth of Sam, our champion

Australian. Every hour you work, there are 30 minutes of it working to line James's pockets rather than your own. In a world without James and his Mates you could retire fifteen years earlier, enjoying the fruits of your labour, rather than watching James enjoy them.

While we focus on James's recent rise in Australia, his Game is eternal. We can never wash ourselves of him completely, for after each purge, he rises again. We will never rid ourselves entirely of those trying to use politics and bureaucracy for private gain, for we all succumb to the temptation: there are countless wannabe Jameses. His position is admired. Many of us send our sons and daughters to the right schools in the hope of befriending James, marrying James or becoming another James. This admiration is misplaced. He is robbing us while pretending that he deserves his spoils, which is despicable, no matter how smartly he plays it.

James is running amok with his Game now in Australia. But Western countries have historically gone through many waves of cleansing themselves of their own Jameses. James's Game was up in Britain in the Glorious Cromwellian revolution of the seventeenth century that abolished many of the privileges the Jameses of the preceding era had assembled. And again, his Game was up in Britain in the early nineteenth century when the wheat barons, who had increased the prices of wheat in the United Kingdom by blocking imports, were dethroned. Many Jameses lost out in the Thatcher era of the 1980s in the United Kingdom, and the Bob Hawke years in Australia, as political reforms took away past privileges.

It has been almost 30 years since the last purges in Australia. James has taken full advantage of the fact that our attention was on other things: family, work, sports, celebrities, Covid and the general business of getting on with life.

The reason we must repeat history again now is that our societies do not notice James at first, for that is his skill. While the rest of us are productive, James and his Mates are organising our poverty by taking advantage of the opportunities we inadvertently leave them. We only become aware of his Game after decades, when his Game becomes so flagrant, entrenched and costly, that it can no longer be ignored.

Economist and social scientist Mançur Olson described the process of social decay resulting from what we call the Game of Mates as 'institutional sclerosis'. He observed that over time all institutions succumb to the power of special interest groups, which incur great economic cost on the community as they reallocate wealth towards themselves. So grossly inefficient is this process that these special interests will impose costs on others that 'exceed the amount redistributed by a huge multiple' (Olson, 1965; Olson, 1982). This means that the scale of the economic loss is staggering because not only does James steal from the economic pie, he spills more crumbs on the floor than he gets himself.

Put another way, it is like James stealing a television from Sam's house, then burning down the house as well!

The late stages of such declines have been called 'elite overproduction' by the historian Peter Turchin (2007). The overall economic pie starts to decline as too much effort goes into grabbing from the pie and too little in creating it: too many Jameses scrambling over what too few Sams are producing. Societies reach a crisis point in which it becomes clear to the majority, even many Jameses, that the whole country is in decline because of rampant corruption and that it is time to enter a reform cycle. Such a crisis period can be postponed by having lots of resources walk into the country with very little effort, such as by wealthy and skilled immigrants coming in without the country having to pay for their education, or by selling easy-to-extract natural resources. Yet the general tendency for more and more Jameses to take a bigger and bigger cut from the national pie unless they are stopped inexorably moves the system towards a crisis. Easy money flowing from outside merely postpones and then intensifies the crisis. Then, societies either socially break down, if Sam chooses to ignore the Game (or plays it themself), or the country gets purged from James's Game, if Sam revolts against it.

It is time once again to look up, take stock of how much the latest generation of Jameses have cost us, spoil their Game and get on with life.

We see reasons for hope. Western countries like ours are far better off now than 100 years ago, and far better off still than 200 years ago. In the long run, we are winning. Australia also has an advantage in these periodic battles against James, for it is an extremely wealthy, well-educated and cooperative society. If any country can rise up and fight their Jameses, it is us. We hope this book can help in this fight by providing the tools to see James's Game, and showing how much it costs Sam, the typical Aussie.

How can we stop James and his Game of Mates in Australia? Our basic advice is to charge James for the privileges he trades in his Game. We should charge him for the value increases on his land and property from public policy decisions. Charge the banks he owns for the profits made by collusion. Charge his mines for the value taken out of the ground. Charge him proper taxes.

Though this won't solve the Game forever, such changes will ensure that James has a hard time stealing from Sam next time he is on the rise.

Another main alternative is to establish a public competitor to supply the product James sells to reduce his collusive power. Set up a state superannuation fund like other countries do, to compete with private ones. Or a state bank. James thrives on a lack of competition, so let's give him some!

A deeper counter-move is to make the whole government bureaucracy harder to influence by money and more tied to the interests of the population. One way to do that would be to have the top bureaucrats appointed by juries made up of randomly selected citizens rather than by elected politicians. This democratises the top of the bureaucracy, making it less dependent on money and politics because the average citizen who happens to spend an unexpected few weeks on a citizen jury is much harder for special interests to reach and corrupt than politicians who spend years working their way to the top, needing money and influence to get there.

It sounds simple, but as you will see, knowing exactly how James plays his Game will reveal that it will not be simple. James will protest and, as we have personally discovered, will play dirty.

Journalists who wanted to report our published research in the areas of property development and infrastructure projects had their jobs threatened. James will tell bald-faced lies. One favourite lie is that there already is intense competition in their market—a favourite line of banks and pharmacies, for example. When pushed, James will enact reforms, but twist them again in his favour, to ensure any change is superficial or indeed hides his Game deeper in the complexities of legalese. He may introduce more bureaucratic rules for land rezoning, for example, something he knows how to navigate and others do not. James and his Mates will kick and scream, as all the Jameses before them have done through the centuries.

Despite the light tone, this book is a touch academic and a bit nerdy. We cannot help this because James is cunning. The only reason he is successful is because his Game is just complex enough to fool most of the people most of the time. That is how he gets away with it.

We will look at the recent history of major economic sectors that reflect some of the main costs of life in Australia, pointing out the nature of the Game of Mates occurring behind the scenes. We cannot give you precise figures for how much the Game costs you in each sector, but we do offer some ballpark estimates based on years of our own research and that of others. We will also discuss the most promising ways to improve our institutions and our laws and reject some popular alternatives that are unlikely to work.

Along our tour of the major sectors of Australia we will tease out the four main elements that make up the Game. First are the flaws in our laws and regulations that leave highly valuable 'grey gifts' on the table that James can snatch for his Mates. Second is the group of allies, or Mates, that forms to capitalise on grey gifts through a network of implicit favour-trades. The third ingredient is a way to signal loyalty to the group of Mates, creating a way for new members to join and for the group to rid itself of traitors. The last ingredient in the Game is the set of myths that shields the actions of James and his Mates from public scrutiny. These myths twist reality in a way to suggest that James's dodgy dealings are in fact good for society.

Seeing these fundamental elements of the Game helps us to narrow down what sort of policy changes can effectively combat the Game, and what popular policy ideas simply play into James's hands. It also helps us to avoid seeing a conspiracy where there is none. We show that the implicit coordination of James and his Mates is a natural human tendency, and one that we are all tempted to play along with, given the opportunity.

We also point out the consequences of the Game of Mates on life in Australia, showing how the large increase in private school education has everything to do with more people trying to muscle in on the Game, and how high immigration and a 'Big Australia' is all about the economic interests of James, not Sam. We will argue that James's Game impoverishes our media, as James's opinions buy airtime. In short, we show how the average Australian is being lulled into the fantasy that James is a good guy whose activities benefit them, rather than belittle and rob them.

In our endeavour, we build on the work of thousands of economists and other researchers who have studied this Game in

Australia and elsewhere. As a group of public-oriented academics and intellectuals, we are watching this Game, analysing it and passing on the torch of fighting it, hoping some of the readers will take their turn and do their bit.

Our approach differs from previous work on the broad topic of inequality and favouritism in Australian political life, like the informative books by Menadue and Keating (2015), Leigh (2013) and Schwab (2010). Rather than trace the dodgy shenanigans of a few insiders or wax lyrical about political ideologies of our times, we focus on the nuts and bolts of the Game and what we should do about it. We explain why we think that more regulation often exacerbates the situation, as James thrives on regulation and is highly adept at getting it to work for him. Simple-sounding solutions, like 'more transparency', are equally useless in most of the sectors we look at. To see why this is so, it is crucial to understand that James is not a solitary individual who finds a corruptible politician but is a networker, able to forge coalitions with many individuals involved in different parts of the system, leading to a Mafia-type hold on individual sectors. This cannot be overcome by adding to the rules that his Mates enforce.

While we give examples from all over Australia and look at the major sectors of the Australian economy, a disproportionate share of stories come from our hometown of Brisbane. That is more a reflection of where we ourselves were exposed to the Game rather than the distribution of wrongdoing across Australia; James does not respect state boundaries.

2
The Great Property Development Game

One of the core powers of government is to establish private property rights in land. It is therefore no surprise that, quite literally, Australia's first James to play the Game of Mates shifted the power of government in his favour to snare highly valuable private property rights in land.

It was 22 February 1790 when James Ruse was granted Australia's first parcel of private land by Governor Arthur Phillip. His 30 acres (12 hectares) was recorded as No. 1 on the Land Grants register and sits in the heart of Parramatta.

Born in Cornwall, England, and raised a farmer, James Ruse came to the penal colony of New South Wales as a convict on the First Fleet in 1788. Ruse lobbied for a release from his sentence and a land grant based on his farming abilities.

> [Governor Phillip] placed Ruse—pending the receipt of the papers from England—upon an acre of cleared and

prepared land on the right bank of the Parramatta River, where the town now stands. A hut was built for him; seeds, implements of agriculture, and a small quantity of livestock were provided; and he was allowed clothing and provisions for twelve months from the public store. As a spur to his industry, he was promised that if he behaved well he would receive a grant of thirty acres on the site where his hut stood. (Britton, 1894)

And James did behave well in that year, for that was his only real choice. Like many Games, what began as a socially beneficial trade, in this case land for farming services, evolved into a relationship where the discretion over the allocation of resources of society led to repeated favour exchanges. Governor Phillip's power came from being able to choose who was awarded land grants, when they were awarded, who was granted better lands and their obligations to the colony. And he exercised that power by repeatedly granting James Ruse the king's land free of charge.

Five years after arriving as a prisoner, James sold the first 30 acres granted to him just three years earlier for £40. At the time, the average yearly wage of an adult male in England was about £26 (Clark, 2011). A year later in January 1794, James Ruse was granted another 140 acres (57 hectares) by the governor. Then another 16 acres (6 hectares) in June 1797. In early 1798 he sold these lands for £300, or about eleven years' wages for an English worker at the time. In 1819, then 60 years old, Ruse obtained another grant of 100 acres (40 hectares) at Riverstone. Altogether, James was given about twenty years' wages in land value in his lifetime by the governor. In today's terms, that is about $1.6 million.[2]

While many other convicts received favourable land grants, they were given different parcels, at different times, with absolute discretion by the governor. Few got as much as James. Ruse made the necessary moves to shift his alliance from the convicts, many of whom organised to undermine attempts by officers to establish order and plundered attempts at farming, to the officers, with years of work establishing trust through his good behaviour and farming skill. Many convicts later followed this path.

These days, this task of signalling trust and reputation is more sophisticated, but fundamentally The Great Property Development Game is the same—property owners seek out favours for themselves above others. This can be in the form of local public investment, like roads and rail, that increases their property value, and rezoning decisions that provide them additional valuable property rights to develop to new uses.

Before we look at The Great Property Development Game in the twenty-first century, let us take another brief diversion to 1911, just ten years after Australia was established as a federation. The battle for the capital city was lost by both Sydney and Melbourne, and the quest for a new location for the nation's capital had begun.

Melbourne had been through a major land boom and bust in the 1880s and 1890s, as had much of the Western world, an episode that led to a shift in thinking about land rights and their role in the rising inequality of the era. Thanks in part to charismatic American political economist Henry George, the public had begun to question the coexistence of progress and poverty, and an influential political movement sprang up around George's call for a single tax on land to remove the unearned gains from land speculation. His argument was that, since land rights are granted from the public at large, private owners should be obliged to rent land at market rates from the state, which can then share the wealth widely. This idea would come to influence how Australia's new capital city, Canberra, was funded, and how the land title system in the Australian Capital Territory (ACT) would function for the next century.

To fund the new buildings, roads and other improvements necessary to establish a capital city worthy of a new great southern nation, the ACT would not play the land grants game that Governor Arthur Phillip had played. Instead, land would be held by the ACT government, and private landholders would be granted leases of up to 99 years on the land and be obliged to pay a market rent annually to the government. In this way, certain private land speculators could not be favoured by the government, nor could they reap massive gains from the mere ownership of land. If James Ruse had been a settler in Canberra in the 1920s, instead of a convict in the 1790s, he could not have received twenty years' wages as a gift from the governor. Those gains would have accumulated to the government, reducing the tax burden on others.

The land titles system in Canberra has worked remarkably well, even though it was never implemented as perfectly as it was planned. Land rents were not adjusted frequently enough to avoid speculation in the land market, and landholders made speculative gains by reselling their leases that had annual rental obligations far below the current market rate.

A main way the ACT government limits the Game of Mates in property is that when it allows a change of use of a land lease, such as from a single residential dwelling to a multi-unit dwelling, the government charges the land leaseholder a betterment tax of 75 per cent of the difference in land value that arises from being able to undertake the higher value use. This 'change of use charge' was introduced in 1971 and has been running for half a century. In 2015, this charge raised about $20 million in revenue. In other states these millions would have gone straight to the pockets of land developers who take all the gains from rezoning. The same principle applies to converting rural to urban land, with the ACT running a government organisation that converts land to urban uses and sells it at market prices, taking on the role of land developer, and reaping 100 per cent of the value gains from that process. This activity generated a $163 million net return to the government in 2014–15 (Murray, 2016a).

Understandably, the Jameses of our era who play The Great Property Development Game like to avoid comparisons with the ACT by pointing out that their leasehold land titles system is somehow fundamentally different. In truth, the only difference between the states and the ACT is that land titles there have a 99-year limit, rather than existing in perpetuity. Even within the ACT, the leases are all but guaranteed to be rolled over for another 99 years, incurring only a small administrative charge.

Apart from that, the administrative systems are almost the same in the different states, and land leaseholders in the ACT have an almost identical bundle of legal rights as landowners in other states. Nowhere do landowners have absolute rights to do with their land whatever they please, because it is important everywhere to regulate what people can build on their land and how much of a nuisance they can be to their neighbours. The very existence of zoning rules shows that indeed there remain public rights held over private land by governments everywhere in Australia.

The ACT got lucky. Its land system was created at a time when a massive depression in the 1890s had led to a political mood that had turned against the trading of favours among the politically active landowning class. Without the free gifts of land from the public at large, the Game of Mates had no reason to get started in the ACT, whereas even in Victoria, where the land bust of the 1890s was most severe, it never truly stopped, despite a wave of public anger and attention. Luck aside, the ACT example shows that it is much easier to avoid letting a Game of Mates start in the first place, than stopping it once it is deeply embedded in the political and social structures of a region.

The current problem

In the twenty-first-century Game of Mates, the value of property rights able to be given through planning and zoning decisions is bigger than ever. The Game is now so entrenched in the social and political structures that a reasonable observer might think another economic depression is the only chance at changing it.

Our modern James is not the rich old grumpy type, or the spoilt young brat you might imagine. He starts out as an enthusiastic young idealist in the public service, with all the ambition to do good things for society that one could expect. James gets involved in town planning departments, spending time negotiating with developers whose applications for approvals hit his desk thick and fast for years. James knows his role is to filter out the nonsense and approve those that make sense for society.

Over time James is invited to attend industry events, grand openings of new buildings and private meetings where he becomes privy to the deep inner workings of the property development industry. Those dribs and drabs of favours—a dinner here, a lunch there, an inside peek—generate a degree of trust, making James begin to identify as a member of the developer 'in-group'. How can anyone maintain their independence when this group of developers is courting them at every turn?

Our James takes up a job offer with one of those developers. How could he refuse? They have spent years telling him how his talent is being wasted in the public service, and he figures it is his chance to do good by working on the inside. He now also has good relationships with his previous colleagues at the planning department, and proceeds to nurture those relationships—after all, they believe they are on the same team and that James is just trying to do good from inside the industry.

After the years James has spent earning his reputation as a property developer who can work cooperatively with the regulatory authorities, his connections in the state planning department pull him aside one day to see if he wants to come back. They are starting a new group that would become an 'elite planning delta force', with great powers to determine zoning controls across the state. They believe they need someone who has worked on both sides of the regulatory fence—inside the government and within industry—and can therefore negotiate positive outcomes for the community. No longer is it us versus them. The authorities and the developers want to be a team.

James's first act as leader of the planning delta force is to approve a planning application for his previous employers, one that he personally worked on for five years without success. He sees the fact that he was asked to be part of the planning delta force as evidence that his earlier work was socially beneficial. It would be negligent not to now use his power to approve his own planning application. This decision provides a gift of property rights to his former employer worth around $25 million. James pretends that this economic reality has not clouded his decision.

James uses his role to great effect. He is in the business of planning for development, and his experience in the development industry had provided him with many contacts who need government cooperation to get their proposals off the ground. In his tenure, James grants many approvals that conflict with the town plans of councils. James has come to believe that council decisions are based on amateur and inappropriate town plans that only serve to constrain developers. That the council's plans might represent the interests of Sam in no way crosses his mind.

When the government ultimately dissolves the planning delta force, James is offered work with one of the developers whose land he had approved for development just a few years earlier. He has jumped the fence again, but by now, there is no fence. Government agencies are full of other Jameses just like him who have done their time with the local developers, and are rotating in and out of government with surprising regularity. In twenty years, James and his Mates have established a Game so entrenched that any regulatory barriers have been dismantled in the interests of ensuring that a connected group of Mates can use the powers of government to grant favours to each other with ease. During this process, they have hidden their economic interests behind a well-orchestrated marketing campaign aiming to convince Sam of the myth that zoning and planning is to blame for high home prices. And none of it is illegal.

You might think we exaggerate. Unfortunately, this is not the case.

The above example of James's revolving-door career fits any number of people. For example, the very real Paul Eagles walked through the revolving door from the developer Lendlease to head up a new Queensland state land development authority in 2007. And Paul is not alone in the revolving-door property development Game, which is now a widespread, legal, and totally normal, part of property sector, despite the obvious perception of inherent conflicts of interest (Murray and Frijters, 2016). Former Queensland premier Campbell Newman did later work with Springfield Land Corporation as did Jim

Varghese, former director general of multiple state government departments who went immediately on to become the Springfield CEO for four years. Former Queensland planning minister Terry Mackenroth, who was investigated for impropriety in some of his planning decisions as minister, retired from politics to sit on the board of Metro, a property development company run by David Devine. Former Brisbane lord mayor Jim Soorley also worked as a lobbyist, with Devine as a client.

In New South Wales, Eddie Obeid was first a property developer before entering the political world to abuse his power as a member of parliament on multiple occasions to improve the value of property and mining interests owned by his family and friends. Of all the players in The Great Property Development Game, Obeid is the only one who has faced any form of punishment, ultimately convicted of misconduct while in public office in late 2016 and sentenced to five years in prison.

The list could go on. Every state has its story of Jameses in property development, and in Queensland the Jameses are at the very top of the political game.

A brazen inside view of how James goes about his Game in property development is in the biographical self-help book of land developer Maha Sinnathamby, ghost-written by Karen McCreadie (2012), called *Stop Not Till the Goal is Reached*. It regales us with stories of how he successfully charmed politicians to get unprecedented and generous development approvals, later partnering with some in private business arrangements, and getting new roads built to his property paid for by the public purse against initial opposition to his 'out of sequence development'.

Especially revealing is how Sinnathamby recalls his use of lawsuits to avoid paying construction companies who were threatening to sue for overdue payments from him back in 1998:

They [Sinnathamby and his business partner Bob Sharpless] needed to make a pre-emptive strike and issue a writ for underperformance before the supplier's writ for non-payment reached them. The plan was simple: sue first. The matter would then be referred to mediation, which would buy them some time until the new year. If they didn't stop this in its tracks it could set off a chain reaction that would eventually bring everything crashing down. Although the tactic was distasteful to both men, they felt they had no choice. Business has its ugly moments and this was one of them.

More recently he has used threats of legal action to make life difficult for nosy journalists who were asking too many questions about his favourable treatment when it comes to major public road and rail investments, which we know from first-hand experience.[3]

The fact that Sinnathamby could proudly write about such exploits tells you that James is currently winning.

The catch is that most of these people are not necessarily acting illegally. In the strict legal sense, they are usually not corrupt. In fact, they often get the laws written for them, entrenching what should be corrupt activity as the normal way of doing business. Australia's rules surrounding conflicts of interest, cooling-off periods for politicians working in industry and the way political discretion can be exercised are also weak. And often the Game of Mates need not rely on the involvement of senior politicians at all, as the more mundane bureaucratic layers of government departments and regulatory agencies can be captured by the Game independently.

The Leppington Triangle case shows this in action. In July 2018 the Australian government purchased a 12 hectare triangular parcel of land adjacent to the new Western Sydney airport in Bringelly. Though independently valued multiple times to be worth $3 million, the landowner was paid $30 million by the department. More puzzling was that instead of using compulsory acquisition powers and compensating at market prices, the department decided to tempt the unwilling seller with a large cash payment. In the auditor's review of this case, they found various potential conflicts of departmental staff, subtle discretion used at various levels, such as defining a boutique valuation methodology to be applied to the land that would create an abnormally high price, and that heads of departments and ministers were not fully briefed on the process. In 2021, Australian Federal Police investigators found no evidence of a crime. A classic case of how subtle institutional capture can be, despite no finding by the AFP investigation of any outright illegal conduct (Evans, 2021).

There is also an enormous degree of mythology and self-delusion that accompanies The Great Property Development Game. Many Jameses genuinely believe that there is no alternative, and that if developers do not get favourable rezoning and planning decisions that no housing will be built. A brief glance at reality tells you this is not true; rezoning decisions do not come with any obligation to develop.

In our previous example, while Paul Eagles was at the helm, the Urban Land Development Authority rezoned the land of his former employer Lendlease in 2010, after years of unsuccessful lobbying. In its planning applications, the company crowed about the urgent demand for the new housing it would build, while at the same time telling its investors in company reports that it didn't plan to build most of the homes for at least two decades to maximise their return. Rather than speeding up development, the Game of Mates slows it down.

The smartest Jameses in the Game even avoid the risks of building homes themselves, simply reselling their land with valuable zoning to the less-connected developers to build new homes on. They specialise in trading on their connections, rather than building new housing.

Quite apart from giving away community wealth to private individuals, handing out rezoning favours without obligations to develop has the additional disadvantage of leading to land speculation. Governor Arthur Phillip expressed such concerns just six months after his arrival in Australia when he was establishing the conditions of granting of land to convicts and officers. 'Lands granted to officers or settlers will, I presume, be on condition of a certain proportion of the lands so granted being cultivated or cleared within a certain time, and which time and quantity can only be determined by the nature of the ground and situation of the lands . . .' (Beck and Jeffery, 1897).

The ACT system is the only one in Australia that counteracts this type of land speculation by having rules that new land leases must be used for the purpose specified on that lease within two years. If the land is not developed, the lease can be cancelled and ownership of the land returned to the government. This is another way the ACT curbs the speculation and favouritism that is rife in town planning and development in the other states.

What it costs you

We know quite well how the Game of Mates is played in property development, and what it costs Sam, because we undertook the largest ever study on which landowners gained favourable rezoning and planning approvals. This work was published in 2016 in the *Journal of Urban Economics*, leading to great national media interest.

We looked at a sample of 1137 landowners from a selection of rezoning decisions in Queensland, and data on a social network with 13,740 entities and 272,810 relationships derived from corporate records, lobbyist records, political donations data and other sources.

We compared similar plots of land that were adjacent to, or across the road from, zoning boundaries, and found that the best indicator of where that boundary would be drawn—which would determine which landowners were given a windfall gain—was the landowner's connectedness in the social network. Other studies have shown that this type of connectedness is the same characteristic that determines which Mafia members earn the most money (Mastrobuoni, 2015). The in-group dynamics of favour-trading that exist in the Mafia and determine how gains are shared amongst the group are very much like the social structure of political favouritism. In our study alone, we found that James and his Mates captured a gift from the public of $410 million between 2007 and 2012 in just our small sample of planning decisions.

For the public at large, the Sams of Australia, what does The Great Property Development Game cost them over a lifetime?

One estimate of the cost to Sam can be established from our own study in Queensland, where we found that around 70 per cent of the value gain from rezoning went to politically connected property developers, leaving only 30 per cent to others. If this would be a representative number, it would imply that in terms of a return on public planning decisions, Sam only gets 30 per cent of the actual return, with 70 per cent usurped by James.

We can also look at the situation a different way to estimate the national size of the favours given away by using the example of the ACT system. We simply ask: if all states had the ACT system of selling new land and charging for new development rights, how much of the wealth that James and his Mates are currently earning would be captured by the public? Of course, we cannot get exact estimates, but it is important to have a ballpark figure in mind.

To estimate this, we take a snapshot from the 2018–19 financial year and look at the revenue of the ACT government from betterment charges and sales of new land leases. Then we scale up this amount to account for price and quantity differences of new dwellings between the ACT and the capital cities of states, which is where most of the gifts of land rezoning take place.

In 2018–19, the ACT made $410 million out of its betterment charges and new land leases. The ACT is a small territory compared to the much bigger states in the rest of Australia, with merely 1.5 per cent of the total population of Australia. Table 1 shows how the ACT system would provide public revenues for the rest of Australia, by adjusting revenues gained in the ACT by the number of dwellings and their prices in other capital cities, holding all other factors constant.

For example, in Perth the average dwelling sold for $436,000, about 30 per cent less than the average dwelling in Canberra, which means Perth has a price ratio relative to Canberra of 0.7. In 2018–19, there were 16,387 new dwellings in Perth, which was 3.4 times more than in Canberra. Combining those two ratios means that, in Perth, the government could have collected an estimated $993 million in additional revenue if it had the same land and zoning system as the ACT.

Doing this simple calculation for the whole country suggests there was $19 billion up for grabs in 2018–19, which went mostly to James and his Mates and meant that the rest of us had to cough up that much more in other taxes and charges.

This example provides obvious clues as to what can be done to combat The Great Property Development Game. The first measure is to remove the economic value of the 'grey gifts' of rezoning. In the ACT system there remains some degree of discretion about how the zoning of the city evolves, but there is much less economic value attached to it, as land leaseholders

Table 1: **Scaling revenues from the ACT land and zoning system**

	Capital city ($)	Trend private	Price ratio	Dwelling ratio	Total mark-up	Revenue ($m)
ACT	604,000	4,882	1.0	1.0	1.0	410
New South Wales	805,000	73,420	1.3	15.0	20.0	8,218
Northern Territory	389,000	768	0.6	0.2	0.1	42
Queensland	492,000	39,008	0.8	8.0	6.5	2,669
South Australia	428,000	11,942	0.7	2.4	1.7	711
Tasmania	459,000	2,691	0.8	0.6	0.3	172
Victoria	635,000	64,953	1.1	13.3	14.0	5,735
Western Australia	436,000	16,387	0.7	3.4	2.4	993
Total						18,950

must pay to utilise their land for higher value uses. Adopting the ACT system of charging for zoning improvements nationally would remove the economic value from planning decisions. Unfortunately, because James and his Mates now control the very political and governmental organisations that would need to support this move in many states, resistance will be immense.

However, politicians do not seem to realise there are vast benefits for them as well if they adopt the ACT system. The main political benefit of taking away the 'honey pot' is that the government can get the honey. The temptation of an extra $19 billion of revenue per year might be enough to tempt a critical mass of politicians to put top-down pressure on their departments and planning authorities to seek out ways to capture these gains. It will be very hard for the Jameses to pretend that taxing their gains will lead to disaster, or that it cannot be done, when there is a working example in the nation's capital.

Indeed, Sydney introduced a betterment levy of 30 per cent of the value gains from converting rural to urban uses in 1970, which was removed in 1973 after pressure from landowners. It raised $9 million in less than three years.[4] And São Paulo, Brazil, began a different system in 2004, with auctions held to sell to landowners the rights to construct additional density, called certificates of additional construction potential, raising almost US$1 billion in five years (Sandroni, 2010).

We were heartened to see the Victorian government adopt in late 2021 their Windfall Gains Tax to recoup for the public a maximum of 50 per cent of the private value allocated by planning decisions. The trick now is to ensure that it persists and does not see the same fate as Sydney's betterment levy from the 1970s, which was reversed after a single electoral cycle by the same conservative government that introduced it in 1969 due to the backlash from powerful landowners (Archer, 1976).

Be warned that James will defend his gains any way he can, and the law is just another tool in his arsenal. When our initial research broke into the media in Queensland and Australia, we were surprised that we did not personally receive angry lawyer letters, or threats from property developers, considering the size of the favours we were exposing. But some of the journalists who quoted us were not so lucky. Several journalists were 'put on notice' by political insiders and threatened with legal action when quoting our findings. We are also aware of two other journalists in south-east Queensland who have been told by their superiors to stop asking questions following their coverage of the Game played by property developers.[5]

If more Australians demand a fairer system, James will feverishly promote the myths that have so far sheltered his Game from public scrutiny. So, the second measure to be taken is to combat these myths wherever they appear. Even in the ACT, the property development industry continues to lobby to remove charges on landowners for being granted higher value uses, despite the half-century of success. The role of the academics, public intellectuals, policy analysts, think tanks, journalists and others with a public platform must be to call out the myths wherever they appear.

A combination of years of our own lobbying and multiple anti-corruption investigations into zoning decisions by several institutions have enabled small steps to be taken in Victoria. It can be done.

But it will take public anger before substantial change comes. A massive economic depression in the 1890s was required to trigger public anger and shift social expectations in a way that allowed the ACT to be formed the way it was, and even that public anger could not then overturn the situation in Victoria or in New South Wales. The depression revealed the way landowners were protected from the widespread poverty experienced by wage earners, and a political movement headed by a charismatic public intellectual Henry George, who spoke clearly about this issue, sprang up. And still such change was only successful locally. In an ideal world, this type of human toll would not be required to trigger a backlash at the Game of Mates.

Another way to curb the excesses of James and his Mates in The Property Development Game is to add sand to the gears of the Game. This can be done by placing controls on personnel movement through the revolving door between planning departments, politics and property developers, and improve the transparency of this behaviour. As we have seen, it is common for politicians to walk out of public office and into jobs at major property developers just months later. The weak current rules about cooling-off periods that require politicians not to work as consultant lobbyists should be extended to apply to in-house lobbyists as well, and for longer periods of time.

Similarly, the revolving-door cycle can be broken by involving outsiders in key decisions. Government reviews of town planning rules could be undertaken with senior staff from outside the state, even outsourced to foreign planning professionals to get objective assessments, rather than the opinions of James and his Mates.

A more radical method to break the hold that James has on the top positions in government planning departments is to have the top of those departments directly appointed by the population via the use of juries of random citizens. When random citizens decide who gets a top job, they will do so with their own interests and those of the rest of the population in mind, not James's interests. Juries of random citizens can of course make mistakes and appoint incompetent people, but that is also true of appointment by politicians, which we have now. With appointment by citizen juries, the relationship between money and the top of the bureaucracy can be broken.

These changes seem simple enough on the surface, but James and his Mates have $19 billion a year in windfall economic gains that they risk losing should the social mood turn against them. They will go down kicking, screaming and litigating. Just as they will in other sectors.

3
The Great Transportation Game

One of the biggest investments a country makes is in its transport infrastructure. Around $12 billion a year is spent in Australia on road and rail projects alone. Prior to the 1990s, government departments and public bodies, including public construction companies, built most of the nation's transport infrastructure. Their projections of how many people would use the roads and rail lines that they built were on average accurate. Often the infrastructure was paid from public funds, but sometimes governments would charge tolls for roads and bridges under a 'user pays' philosophy, simply because it was an easy source of taxation. Using tolls to raise funds for the authorities is common historically, from the Romans to medieval British kingdoms, and colonial Australia, with Parramatta Road being the first toll road, opening in 1811.[6]

Before the 1990s there were no major problems with the road and rail sector in Australia. In that period, James and his Mates were more active when it came to airlines and ports. James eventually figured out that there was an opportunity to play the Game in transport because at the end of the day, nearly all infrastructure decisions are made by politicians who have discretion about which projects get built, who gets large construction contracts and under what conditions those contracts are written. If only James and his Mates could use that discretionary power to their advantage, they could cash in at the expense of Sam.

Because transport investments had been made so successfully by government departments and public agencies for decades, James needed a myth that could provide cover from public scrutiny as he sought out his Mates to learn how, together, they could get a cut of this sector of the economy. His goal was clear: to own roads and other infrastructure that would be worth a lot more than it cost him to build, preferably paid for by government as well.

We have extensively analysed the largest 38 road and rail infrastructure projects since 1992 in Australia, including high-profile projects like the Sydney Harbour Tunnel and the major toll roads in Melbourne, and can tell you how James and his Mates did it. Our research assistant Kathy Ahern has pored over the documents, analysis and reviews, helping to tease out the main elements of how James succeeded in turning a simple idea into a lucrative Game of Mates.

The myth that worked so well for James in this sector, and in many others, was that the government budget is like that of a household, and that governments must 'live within their means' by cutting back spending, no longer borrowing to pay for new road and rail construction. The story was that government debts would have to be paid by future generations and future Sams should be free of such obligations. The supposed solution that accompanied the myth was to let the private sector fund costly infrastructure projects, and in return give them ownership for many decades with the right to charge tolls and other fees to users.

James's opportunity lay in understanding much better than the public how to manipulate the measurement of public debt: James saw a way to make it appear as if his involvement lowered public debt whilst in fact increasing it. Think of it from his point of view.

What if James could hide the public debt involved in infrastructure investments so that people wouldn't see that in fact future generations were still going to pay for new infrastructure? What if he could bind governments into contracts where he himself would pay almost nothing, but make it appear on the government books that he was paying for it, allowing politicians to brag that they were investing in large infrastructure projects without paying for it? Would the population be naive enough to believe that private companies were 'partnering' with government for the benefit of the public? If James and his Mates in government could keep to the story that they were doing the public a favour, they thought they would get away with it.

And they did.

The basic strategy was to keep the costs of building infrastructure from appearing as public debt. In our analysis of 38 cases, there were numerous accounting tricks that kept coming up.

- Private companies would appear to put their own money at risk to build a piece of infrastructure, such as a toll road, but governments would in fact guarantee a high return on their investment, even if only few people used the infrastructure once it was built. This trick binds future populations into paying James via taxation if tolls are insufficient to meet this return, which is identical to what happens when governments borrow money by issuing bonds. The guaranteed return is a future 'liability' of the public but, crucially, it is not counted as public debt in official statistics and thus allowed governments to claim James was paying for the infrastructure.

- With the guarantee in hand, James could simply borrow from banks, or from abroad. The same debt was made and was guaranteed to be paid off by the government, but it was not on the books as public debt. To all practical purposes, the infrastructure was still financed by the government and the public, but now at inflated prices and with a guarantee of large profits to James. Since the guaranteed rates of return were extortionately high (sometimes 15 per cent or more), these arrangements were invariably much more expensive for the public than 'normal' debt-financed infrastructure.

- Private companies would often not actually put up much private money but would borrow money from the government itself at low interest rates which they only would have to pay back if they exceeded a certain return later. The government itself could then borrow the money to make this contribution. The crucial element that made this trick work politically is that a public loan to a private company can be counted as a financial asset on the government's books, netting out any extra debt taken on before being consolidated and reported, even if it is unlikely that it will ever get paid back and earns absurdly low interest rates. For example, the New South Wales government granted a $223 million loan for Sydney Harbour Tunnel that was never paid back, and the arrangement between the Victorian government and Melbourne CityLink Authority has allowed Transurban to dodge its liabilities for payments to the state worth $456 million in 2001 (Odgers, 2002). This astonishing trick essentially amounted to the public paying to build something that James would subsequently own, which should be seen as a straightforward gift of publicly funded infrastructure to James. Unsurprisingly, these arrangements were kept rather quiet at the time they were made.

- The contracts would specify future benefits that James knew would be lucrative, but which did not have an openly announced dollar value, and which could be hidden in legalese so as to not be clear to an outsider. The benefit could be the right to levy tolls for 30 years; it could be a monopoly over future repair contracts on the infrastructure (which gave James an incentive to do a shoddy job in the first place); it could be the guarantee that no other infrastructure would be built that would compete with what James built; it could be exemptions from planning rules such that James could cheaply buy up and use land; it could be the guarantee that governments would take on the risks of flooding or environmental damage (which often is the main risk of cost blowouts), and more. In the

38 cases studied, we have seen many imaginative favours hidden in the nitty-gritty of the contracts that turned out to be worth a lot to James, but which no one but a real expert would have been aware of beforehand.

The common name for these financial arrangements to build infrastructure is public private partnerships (PPPs). These legal arrangements were sold to the public as a win–win partnership between the public and private sector, jointly funding a project beyond what could normally be done by the public alone. It was one of James's most effective myths. Yet the exact opposite was usually the case, with little private money involved, and the public taking all the risk, and James winning no matter what. Most researchers who study this area quickly learn the underlying reality we have described.

> PPPs originated as an accounting trick, a way round the government's own constraints on public borrowing. This remains the overwhelming attraction for governments and international institutions. Just as companies like Enron had tried to conceal their true liabilities by moving them 'off-balance-sheet', so governments started using PPPs as 'tricks . . . whereby public accounts imitate the creative accounting of some companies in the past'. (Hall, 2014)

So much has James's logic been internalised by government agencies that similar accounting tricks are used solely to hide public debt from sight, but not necessarily to benefit James.

In 2020, the New South Wales government converted its agency for rail operations (RailCorp) to a state-owned corporation to shift liabilities 'off book'. This meant that subsidies by the government to the new entity could be badged 'equity injections' rather than expenses, hiding the true economic situation. The Audit Office of New South Wales raised concerns in its 2021 audit, but we expect little political fallout since the public is by and large still ignorant of such deceptions and how they can be used to serve James and his Mates (Hannam, 2021).

James's Game required crafty negotiations before, during and after PPP transport projects were built. James had a strong incentive to claim beforehand that the infrastructure he would build was going to be used a lot, such that toll returns in the future would be high and the public would supposedly not need to compensate him for not getting the guaranteed returns.

Amongst our seventeen official PPPs out of 38 major projects from 1992 to 2015, we found that the average PPP had traffic outcomes that were 40 per cent below forecast, compared to 6 per cent above forecast for publicly built projects. That means that we now live with the legacy of James's inefficiency, with his roads carrying 40 per cent fewer trips than promised before construction, and 46 per cent below what publicly built projects delivered.

There are no prizes for guessing where the systematically over-optimistic estimates came from. James himself supplied them as part of the prospectus and other documents generated at the time of the PPP. These exaggerated traffic and usage forecasts usually came from James's Mates in their role as consulting forecasters.

Cutting new deals in transport meant James needed a group of Mates to coordinate with. PPP deals were often proposed by consortia, involving banks, construction companies, investment funds and middlemen, including former politicians. In some states, like Queensland, James proposed infrastructure without any government agency identifying a need for it. But in other states, like Western Australia, James responded mostly to government assessment of need, though of course that 'assessment of need' simply offered another avenue for James to direct the hand of government.

Asking governments to pay for a part of the project dreamt up by James became so common it was given a name—unsolicited proposals. In a brilliant piece of marketing, that unattractive label has recently been rebadged as 'market-led proposals'.

The consortia often involved the country's biggest banks, Macquarie in particular. The term 'Macquarie model' is infamous, and partly synonymous with a bad deal for the public. Investment banks, retail banks and even superannuation funds were sometimes persuaded to put other people's money at risk in projects that would provide James and his Mates all the benefits.

The deals of course needed the cooperation of James's Mates in political parties and governments, who would pass the legislation necessary to utilise government powers to acquire property, and to delegate power to the PPP entity. Naturally, the financial interests of the Jameses in government were tightly linked to the banks and construction companies that would benefit from PPP projects. And naturally, there were revolving doors between the various people involved. We give examples of this later.

Once the project was up and running, James was quick to use other opportunities to make more money by cementing the value of his piece of infrastructure. For example, when traffic levels in the Cross City Tunnel (CCT) in Sydney were consistently below forecast and revenues were not providing a sufficient return for investors, James called on his Mates to make changes to alternative roads that would funnel more traffic through his tunnel. James wanted to make it difficult for cars to take any other route by artificially creating congestion elsewhere. This funnelling could be done under the pretence of reducing surface road traffic and 'improving the public domain' (Chung, 2008). Another favour, another myth.

However, at least in the case of the CCT, the public did see through the myth and pushed back against the funnelling, leading to the cancellation of many of the planned surface road closures. Nevertheless, the CCT illustrates that PPPs often contribute very little to the overall economic growth of the areas they are in. Often these projects simply cause congestion elsewhere in the road network that requires further public investment to remedy.

Additional favours can also be granted near the end of a PPP deal. James would like to own the infrastructure long past the time he is supposed to own it, and can just suggest to his political Mates that he should own it for longer. Transurban, owners of Melbourne's CityLink toll road, asked for such a favour using a cover story that to us makes little sense (Schneiders and Millar, 2016).

Even under the very best of contractual circumstances, where there are no financial tricks or additional favours along the way,

James can find ways to cheat the public. PPP contracts have an inherent incentive for James to skimp on maintenance, since PPP contracts are typically granted to private ownership for 30 years, and then revert to public ownership. After about twenty years, James has little interest in maintenance or repair beyond what he needs to do to ensure the transfer back to government goes ahead. Also, James could do deals with road maintenance contractors to build the original road with poor materials so that more repairs would be needed after ownership is returned to the public.

The total costs and some examples

We tallied up the potential economic gains if the same amount of money that was spent on PPP projects was spent on projects with similar benefit–cost ratios to the publicly funded ones. Looking at just a sample of 38 major road and rail projects from 1992 to 2015, seventeen of which were PPP projects, we calculated a benefit of $32 billion that we have forgone because James and his Mates sank their teeth into the lucrative transport investment sector.[7]

Where did this estimate come from? We essentially took the promised benefits by James for the PPP projects at face value, meaning that we start by presuming that the $31 billion investment in James's PPP projects should indeed have made a return of around $62 billion. That 2-to-1 ratio is roughly what publicly built infrastructure projects returned in the same period. We then note that the traffic flow was 40 per cent below what James claimed it would be, and what comparable public projects had, meaning that the actual benefits were around $28 billion less than they would have been if their forecasts had been the same as that of publicly built infrastructure.

We then note that publicly built infrastructure even at the outset had a higher expected benefit–cost ratio because of lower overheads and clearer public need, being focused on smaller higher-return projects. If we factor in that perhaps the choice of bigger, lower return projects is part of the Game, there is an additional $4 billion forgone by having PPP projects instead of more publicly built infrastructure, meaning a total $32 billion loss. In terms of the estimated overall benefits from infrastructure, this means the PPPs reduced the benefits by around 50 per cent relative to what it could have been if there were no PPPs.[8]

How much does this loss mean to the average Sam? We can take the $32 billion estimate of forgone economic benefit from 1992 to 2015 from building the wrong transport infrastructure and divide this by the average number of households in that period, to get $3200 per household. These losses are likely to be far higher than the gains to James, which just shows the willingness of James and his Mates to inflict economic damage on Sam if it benefits them. Compared to the advertised total costs of all the 38 infrastructure projects of $60 billion, the $32 billion loss is an additional cost of around 50 per cent. This gives a rough rule of thumb that for every dollar spent on transport infrastructure projects we lose another $0.50 because of James.

As a detailed illustration of the various deceptions at play, consider the Clem7 tunnel in Brisbane. It was constructed by a PPP consortium of Jameses called RiverCity Motorway. The tunnel was promoted as a necessary way to add an additional river crossing to the road network. James argued that his project would generate a fifteen-minute time-saving compared to existing roads, though it delivered less than eight minutes saving in practice. James promised 90,000 trips per day but got only 25,000. James promised a $2 toll. Sam got a $5 toll. Because of this, Brisbane now has an empty tunnel running under congested surface roads—a highly inefficient outcome (Loader, 2016).

To illustrate the ability of James to avoid putting up any of his own money at all, look no further than the ubiquitous use of success fees for Mates who ensure that such deals go ahead. Former Queensland politician Terry Mackenroth and former federal politician Con Sciacca, for example, together earned a $1 million success fee from the proponent of Brisbane's Airport Link PPP a consortium called BrisConnections. In addition, Macquarie Bank made $110 million in upfront fees for arranging the financial affairs for Airport Link.

This example also shows the penchant for key individuals to have multiple roles in these deals. Former investment banker and Labor insider Trevor Rowe was appointed the chair of Bris-Connections at the same time he was chair of the state-owned Queensland Investment Corporation (QIC) (Dunlevy, 2009a). And—would you believe it?—QIC had invested $25 million of the superannuation balances of Queensland public servants in the project, though this decision occurred prior to Rowe's appointment at QIC. This money was almost all lost, and the business ultimately went into receivership and was purchased at a 65 per cent discount on the costs by another group of Jameses,

Transurban. Macquarie Group, who had originally owned an 18 per cent stake in the company, dodged $120 million in losses by selling their equity stake before the price collapsed (Hawthorne, 2009).

A recent deal shows how the evolution of these tricks has become the new normal. Consider the massive public West-Connex toll road in Sydney. Bundled with two other existing motorways, it was sold in a series of deals from 2018 to 2021 to major private road monopolist Transurban, which already owned seven of the nine Sydney toll roads. The state got $20 billion out of the sale, but some analysts suggest that the many promises that are part of the deal mean that the state will give Transurban over $23 billion worth of assets—more than it will get from the sale—on the project. The deal shows all the tricks we have described. For example, it included the right for Transurban to add a toll to the existing M5 West motorway from 2026, giving Transurban a way to fleece Sam in the future for something he thought was already built and paid for. The deal also included a promise by the state to continue a cash-back subsidy scheme for users of the M5 South West, essentially a direct subsidy from the state to Transurban. Much of the deal was hidden from public scrutiny. A new trick that was part of this deal is a clever 'stapled trust' structure that has allowed Transurban to pay no corporate tax for years (Standen, 2018), meaning that any future upside will go to James.

While there was much talk about the anti-competitive issues of creating a private road monopolist in Sydney from the WestConnex privatisation, nothing has been done to stop this.

We fear for Sam that an example has been set that will be copied in future projects, costing Sam billions once again.

Solutions

How can transport investment be done differently? The most promising solution is to go back to how transport was organised before the PPP craze: make it the business of a transport and infrastructure department to determine what transport needs the population has, and then to use public money to build it and maintain it with minimal political interference.

In a more economically sensible environment, transport projects would be selected on their merits in terms of contributing to mobility. To do this, technical experts would consider the whole transport network and determine which new additions give the best bang for the buck. With a list of these projects, from best to worst return, construction would start at the top and work downwards, with new projects being assessed and added routinely. Construction contracts to private companies would be granted through competitive processes, with publicly owned construction companies also participating. The reason to ensure a public alternative in this bidding process is to avoid the situation where only one private bidder materialises, or where the bidders are merely arms of the same construction cartel and implicitly (or explicitly) coordinate to charge higher prices.

Such arrangements are still the norm in many countries, and Australia still has some sidelined transport departments in various states that could resume this role if we decided to. All it needs is the political will to dislodge James and his Mates.

It is also quite simple to get back the money the public has already handed to the PPPs. All it requires is for a government to vigorously pursue and investigate the individuals and companies involved in breaches of various parts of the law, including labour laws, environmental laws and public sector laws around contracts and governance. We are confident that there will be many breaches that can be used as a basis for demanding compensation from James and taking back the gifts that previous governments have promised. All it needs is political will.

4
Grey Gifts

At its core, the underlying power that James co-opted when playing the Game of Mates in property and transportation was the discretion of the politicians and the bureaucrats to make rezoning decisions and determine the content of infrastructure contracts. James's wealth in those sectors came from these discretionary decisions over the allocation of things that have large private value but are not priced. They are 'grey gifts', and they are the currency of 'grey corruption'. In a world with clearly defined rules and no political and bureaucratic discretion, there are no grey gifts. The Game is thus about wriggle room.

The reality is that politicians and top bureaucrats regularly make decisions that have private winners and losers, decisions that can make millionaires out of some and paupers out of others. Their power comes from being able to choose who gets the massive economic value of their grey gifts, all the while not having to bear any personal costs. Instead, Sam bears the costs.

A grey gift is a property right that initially belonged to the public as a whole that is given to particular private parties without fair payment. The decision to allocate a grey gift to particular people rather than to the public as a whole is then invariably an abuse of power entrusted into politicians and bureaucrats who are supposed to represent everyone equally. Only when the benefits of grey gifts are equally available to everybody, or those who get the gift are forced to pay a fair price for it, is there no implicit theft of Sam by James. Only then is political power applied in a neutral manner: that is, without favouritism.

The problem is particularly large if there are frequent decisions that are not well observed by the electorate. Complex, hard-to-read regulatory environments require politicians and top bureaucrats to rely on their judgement and discretion to interpret and enforce the rules. Which way they err can make millions of dollars of difference to the people and companies operating under those rules. In a sense, they control an 'economic honey pot'.

And where there is honey, you attract flies. James and his ilk swarm about to get a taste of millions of dollars on offer from grey gifts. In property, the gift is the right to use land differently. Who gets that property right is decided with a great deal of discretion in the political and bureaucratic system, but outside that system that property right has a market value. In infrastructure, the tax receipts of current and future generations are put in the hands of private owners of infrastructure projects through negotiated, flexible and secretive contractual arrangements, the value of which is capitalised into the value of the PPP companies.

A simple test to help see whether a grey gift is being given is to ask whether the recipient would be willing to pay for the decision if they were made to. Would a developer pay a higher fee to choose their own assessor? Would they pay for rezoning? They would, because in places they are made to, they do.

Would a toll road owner pay to close alternative roadways that compete with it? When the answer is yes, you have identified a grey gift, and in doing so, identified a social environment ripe for the formation of a Game of Mates. This same method of identification provides the first clues about how to combat the Game of Mates—charge the market value of grey gifts to those who benefit. Make James pay!

The cartoon in Figure 1 tries to give you a memorable idea of how to think about grey gifts. The pipework represents the rule systems and institutions in our society, which are set up to invest in future prosperity while sharing the wealth of society broadly, and with some degree of fairness. At the top are the ultimate rule setters, the politicians who have broad control over the legal valves to direct money one way or the other. While they must respond to electoral sensitivities, they do have substantial overall power and discretion as to which laws pass and in what form. The political system is therefore the ultimate controller of the multi-billion-dollar honey pot of the country's economic surplus, both past (tax receipts), present (rights) and future (fees and monopolies). This is why the media and the public take so much interest in their dealings; why we ensure some degree of disclosure of political donations; why we insist on some degree of transparency; and yet why James and his Mates are still so involved in the major parties.

Figure 1: **Discretion in the system leaves grey gifts for James and his Mates**

Because of the degree of public interest in political decisions, political relationships and politicians themselves, the political class responds to this scrutiny by devolving much of its power further down the regulatory pipes to agencies and organisations that get to make decisions about where the money flows, and therefore who gets the grey gifts on offer. Sometimes these are top bureaucrats, sometimes there are 'independent' agencies that themselves make discretionary decisions about which companies will be investigated for fraud (the Australian Securities and

Investments Commission—ASIC), or what regulations will apply to which monopolists (the Australian Competition and Consumer Commission—ACCC).

James tries to direct the decisions of both the top politicians and the bureaucrats in such agencies. If the system works the way it is supposed to, everyone gets an equal share in the benefits, or at least an equal chance to benefit. His task is therefore to get the politicians and bureaucrats who control the flows of economic wealth of society at large through these regulatory pipes by turning the valves in the favour of him and his Mates, rather than Sam.

Notice too that to give a grey gift, those who control the valves are not themselves paying for it. Instead, they are redirecting portions of the whole nation's wealth away from Sam, meaning the value of grey gifts available can be astronomical. Even worse, it is often the case that by trying to funnel the money through the pipes to James, it results in less money getting through the pipes in total. This happens in cases where favouring James is not a choice between equals, but where choosing James provides inferior economic outcomes. We can think of rezoning land for higher-density development that is far from existing infrastructure, rather than closer land owned by Sam. Here society incurs the extra cost of extending road, water, sewerage and power infrastructure that needn't have been built if Sam's land had been rezoned instead. In transport infrastructure, the grey gift to James meant building roads that weren't the most efficient additions to the road network, a complete loss to society.

In the examples we have talked about so far, the highly valuable grey gifts did not always exist at the outset of the Game. They often arise by a mix of chance and the direct activities of potential Jameses. Large rezoning decisions were always discretionary but historically not worth all that much to private owners because price differences between zones were much lower, making the decision-making power much less lucrative. From the point of view of the politicians and James, the increase in value of this gift emerged more or less by accident after the 1980s when property prices close to city centres rose relative to farmland. The price increase meant a lot of money could be directed into particular pockets by ensuring that new rights to build more property on existing land went a certain way. James and his Mates just organised the regulations around rezoning so that the money flowed their way.

The same is true to some extent with PPP infrastructure contracts. Because rezoning and transportation are strongly intertwined, the periods of rapid population growth created the need for more infrastructure in the areas rezoned, which meant there was something valuable to decide upon that was not there before. And in the case of the PPP transport projects, it was James himself who managed to cast the problem of transport investment as a budgetary one, a helpful story that created the opportunity for grey gifts to exist in the complex contract negotiations necessary in PPP projects.

In truly competitive markets, this kind of discretionary control over the things of value to others is tightly limited. Just think about the people working in various layers at McDonald's fast-food restaurants.

For the low-level employees in one of their restaurants, there is almost no discretion because they operate in a world of strict rules and constant monitoring. They can't make a better burger for their friends because all the burgers must be made according to the same rigid protocol. They can't give discounts, and they can't choose suppliers to the restaurants. The low-level employees are like machines. And the reason it is organised like this is to ensure consistency and to avoid the formation of favoured groups within the company who could swarm around grey gifts left in their systems.

The discretionary choices begin to emerge with store managers, whose primary discretion concerns the staff roster. This power allows them to hire their friends and favour particular employees over others, for instance in terms of granting more desirable shift times. If you have been in that situation, you would immediately recognise it as a valuable grey gift that can be traded. There is some monitoring of the manager, but it is always imperfect because the manager's decision-making environment is not known beforehand and can thus not be captured in rigid rules. Higher level managers cannot know who is willing to be an employee and what shift times are more desirable in different places, so they will be forced to trust store managers, giving them some discretionary power to determine winners and losers.

Higher up still and the discretionary power over the allocation of valuable resources starts to increase, with country managers making decisions such as who they prefer to supply large orders of inputs (potatoes, meat) and at what price, where to buy property for new stores, and which firms to involve in marketing. These are huge discretionary decisions worth many millions, an environment ripe for James and his Mates to take advantage of.

But these higher-level McDonald's managers are still very constrained. Fast food is a highly competitive business with many other chains and local restaurants competing for the same customers. In this environment, a manager who repeatedly does favours to others will quickly be spotted as someone who is making a loss for the company and will be fired. If the favours are bad enough and cannot be avoided, it is possible that McDonald's simply pulls out of a country altogether. Such a decision is the discretion of someone even higher up the chain.

Overall, the competition faced by McDonald's from the top all the way down means that it has constructed a system of internal rules to eliminate as many potential grey gifts—the valves that control who gets the surplus the business generates—as possible. Everyone must earn their way in such a competitive industry. The basic reason that the constraints on the discretion of McDonald's managers do not hold in general for politicians and top bureaucrats is that there is no direct competition for government. In our society there is just one government, and any would-be competitor is deemed a traitor. Quite literally, the worst crime there is in our society is to challenge the power of government.

During their time in government, those at the top of the political system, and inside state bureaucracies, do not face the type of competition that McDonald's does. The public cannot choose not to be part of the elected government's rules and choose to obey the rules of an alternative government. Even after the infrequent political competition from elections, opposition political parties who do find electoral success will realise that to stay in power they must appease James, rather than Sam, whose vote got them elected. Over time this leads to an implicit agreement between both sides of politics that electoral competition will avoid issues that take back economic resources from James and give them to Sam. We see evidence for this in political donations data, where most major donors, the Jameses, donate to both sides of politics equally.

This lack of genuine competition in politics, and the existence of discretion, is sometimes desirable because we want politicians to be able to react to new circumstances and take account of local issues, make long-term decisions and represent our broader social values. We put our faith in their judgements, at least for a while.

This idea also tells us in which areas of the economy to expect more grey gifts, and which will hence be more prone to a Game of Mates forming. In resource sectors, where the product is freely provided by nature, who benefits from these resources is always the result of rule systems created by government. These rules will necessarily be imperfect and will always involve the creation of some form of monopoly control over the resources.

Property is likewise a government-granted monopoly, and the PPP arrangements we saw in transport projects are pure discretionary financial negotiations with the public's money on the line. The banking system, to name another major sector, is a government-sanctioned industry providing a public service necessary to underpin economic activity. The way banks are constrained by their interactions with the central bank (the Reserve Bank of Australia) also constrains the ability for new competitor banks to take market share. If an industry is by its nature not competitive, James will find opportunities to extract grey gifts from rule-makers.

The main lesson from our McDonald's example is that, where competition can be facilitated in areas of economic production, it will limit the ability for James to take control. For example, creating publicly owned competitors where possible will pressure the newly competitive private companies to take back grey gifts, rather than trading them away at a cost to their customers, in order to remain in business. It won't work in all cases, and it can be the case that public institutions generate their own costly Games as they make valuable discretionary decisions, but it is an important idea we will revisit later.

It is worth pointing out that there are many areas in public life where politicians have little discretion. Though they are allowed to propose new laws, top politicians are not allowed to inter-fere with ongoing criminal cases and declare someone guilty or innocent of breaking a law. That right belongs to a different group (lawyers and judges) who protect that territory for their own ends. This separation of powers is done precisely to avoid poli-ticians directly freeing their family members and friends, though they can of course still interfere in more subtle ways. Similarly, politicians and top bureaucrats might decide on the curriculum taught in primary schools but can usually not prevent a particular kid from going to a local primary school. Thus, in many areas politicians and bureaucrats set rules that affect everyone similarly and cannot easily make decisions that make a particular person (or small group) very rich or poor.

So, the key aspect to the Game of Mates we have seen in transport infrastructure and property rezoning, and what we will see later in other sectors, is that major favours are given out in a discretionary fashion without the population paying much attention (and hence without much competitive pressure on the politicians to direct the benefits of the favours to the populace). What else can be given away by discretion, you might wonder?

As we will see later, what can be given away includes many other things. Deciding whom to tax and how to spend taxes are prime examples, and much of the public scrutiny of politicians centres on their spending decisions, with many areas, such as education and health, having dedicated ministries arguing for a slice of the pie, as well as many monitoring systems that look at how the money was spent and allocated. This will be of prime interest when we later discuss the Game in health, education and other heavily regulated areas of the economy.

There are many less obvious favours that can be done though, which are much easier to hide from public view. A key one in the case of infrastructure is the right to charge others for something in the future: for instance, toll fees on roads that last for decades. Giving away the right to have high toll fees for the next 30 years is a favour that will only really be noticed by the next generation and is hence a good way to hide just how much has been given away, particularly if the precise arrangements are secret and subject to frequent changes.

Another key favour is granting exclusive rights to provide a product. One example is preventing foreign competitors from selling bananas in Australia, a favour that is worth around half-a-billion dollars a year, as it leads to extortionate banana prices in years with poor harvests (Foster, Frijters and Ko, 2018). Other forms of exclusive rights come from government-granted monopolies (such as in banking) or by subtle restrictions on competition, such as with pharmacies. In Australia, no pharmacist can open within 1.5 kilometres of an existing chemist unless certain conditions are met, a rule that has been crucial in making pharmacies much more expensive than they need to be (we discuss this trick in more detail in later chapters).

What is surprising is that, from the point of view of James, the more complex the regulations and the more agencies officially involved, the easier it becomes to get valuable grey gifts to go his way. It is crucial to understand this when we will talk about solutions, as more rules often work in James's favour.

One main reason James thrives on complicated rules is that it makes the job harder for any would-be competitor. In the jargon of economics, 'compliance is a natural monopoly'. There is a fixed cost in understanding any regulation and once James has paid that fixed cost, the cost of complying many times is minimal. Any newcomer would have to put in a lot of effort to be able to comply. So large compliance costs naturally lead to few competitors. The more complex the rules and the more the rules are subtly changed because of 'consultation' with the people who are still in the Game (i.e., the few left standing), the harder it is for anyone else to compete with James.

A related advantage of complex regulation is that James soon knows more about the regulation and how to circumvent it or use it in his favour than the regulator. If the regulator is particularly honest and competent, James offers them a job. This can help James to know more than the next regulator, or simply gets the honest regulator out of the way and into a more harmless job. As a result of this dynamic, in nearly every major sector we will look at, James probably knows more about the regulations than either the public, the government or the ministers. In banking, the private banks clearly know more about regulation than any regulator. In mining, the miners know more about the regulations relevant to them (environment, taxation, labour laws, etc.) than others. In property zoning, the property developers know far more than we do.

The advantages to James of complex regulation are slow to become apparent. When a new sector is developing, regulators will be ahead of the regulated, and there will be many new entrants trying to keep up. But over time, the few who know best how to play the system survive and get far ahead of the regulators, protected by the complexity of the situation. This means it is often more effective to take away the value of the grey gifts than to add more complexity to the rules supposedly deciding who gets the lucrative gifts.

The complexity of the system works for James in other ways. He does not need to seek out the most popular politicians in order to grasp some power. He can seek out cooperation from lower-level agencies and party elders, building up a power base inside the political parties and bureaucracies that make him a very attractive partner for the top politicians to appease and reward.

In conclusion, the idea of a valuable grey gift as the first ingredient in the Game of Mates helps us to better identify situations where James and his Mates have gained control of the system. We know to look for discretion over decisions that pick winners and losers, and that any statutory body that decides on big winners and losers will itself become a target for James. Taking the honey pot off the table is therefore one of the main actions we propose to combat the Game of Mates.

Let us be clear about our innate sympathies. We are not saying that all businessmen are crooks. Far from it. Most businesses can only marvel at how others are getting unfair advantages from playing the Game of Mates, while they invest and toil away at making better products and attracting customers, only to have to pay more taxes than James and deal with the fact that his activities make other things more expensive (like the currency and vital inputs). Hence, we are definitely on the side of most small businesses and competitive large businesses. They are also the battlers in our country.

In many ways, Sam, the typical Australian who is having their wealth stolen by James and his Mates, is also in business and competes fairly. The Game that James plays avoids competition with Sam by going over Sam's head, co-opting the ultimate monopoly of government.

5
The Great Superannuation Game

Saving for retirement always comes with the question of how we should invest to guarantee we have enough income for a comfortable old age. It is a question that should concern Sam more than James, though it turns out, as you would expect, James calls most of the shots on how Sam saves for retirement.

Australia, like many countries, has addressed the question of how to fund retirement by organising a minimum savings program for everyone in the population. The best of these programs are run by government agencies that invest on behalf of the whole population. Australia does not have such a system. Instead, a public pension system provides a modest minimum level of pension for all below a certain level of wealth and income, while most retirement savings in Australia accrue in privately run superannuation accounts, into which everyone is forced to contribute a minimum amount during their working life. Or more simply, as journalist Ross Gittins describes the scheme: 'the government compels employers to take 9.5 per cent [now 10 per cent] of their workers' wages and hand this over to the "financial services" industry, then looks the other way while these fat cats rip off the mugs the government has delivered into their hands' (Gittins, 2015).

The idea of a competitive superannuation fund market is that customers of funds can make well-informed choices, leading to price competition, weeding out inefficient funds, and increasing overall returns and retirement incomes. But superannuation is not like other markets such as food or clothing. It is a product you are tied to for decades, and customers can never know its value in advance. Comparing products is complex and difficult, even for experts. Sam cannot opt out of the system if there are no funds to their liking and in many sectors Sam is forced to accept their retirement savings going into a particular fund.

People who make choices about their superannuation do so blindly. But James's perspective from the inside of superannuation companies and regulatory bodies is certainly not blind. And it is James who has discretion over how the funds that invest Sam's retirement savings are run, what fees they charge, how they package their products to maximise profits instead of Sam's savings, and how the regulations and tax laws governing superannuation are written.

Back when the compulsory superannuation system was becoming established in the 1980s and early 1990s, led politically by then Labor Treasurer and later Prime Minister Paul Keating, James and his Mates grew alert to a great new opportunity to defraud the general population. You see, James was a union official who recognised that his ability to determine the superannuation fund that the workers in his industry would get to choose was worth gold. It was a grey gift to be traded.

So James set to work. First, he formed friendship groups at the top of his union so that there was no dissent there, bullying and harassing the honest union officials so that they left. Then with his Mates, they set up their own industry super funds, with themselves as managers. He then negotiated with the bosses in that industry who joined the industry super fund as co-directors and together decided that the industry fund they co-owned was to be the main one that was recommended to all workers. Though they initially had to offer their workers some other choices as well, they made sure these other choices were hopelessly expensive and difficult to understand.

Over time, James and his Mates worked their political connections so that the industry super fund they set up was legally recognised as the only fund that workers in that industry could join, becoming a blatant monopoly. Together with other union leaders and industry bosses, they lobbied parliament to avoid attempts at forcing more choice or transparency. On the contrary, they stacked their industry super funds full of hidden fees that emerge when one switches to other funds or tries to withdraw funds to run a self-managed super fund.

And how does James make money out of it? Sneakily, as you might expect. James of course now has an enormous salary and bonus due to his position in the super fund. But he also controls where the funds are invested, being able to offer favours to other groups of Jameses by funding their projects instead of others. We have already seen an example in the world of PPP transport projects where the head of Queensland Investment Corporation (QIC), Trevor Rowe, who managed $1.45 billion of funds on behalf of Sunsuper, lost millions of his members' retirement savings by investing in a questionable road tunnel project that lined the pockets of his Mates. Also, an employee of the lobbying firm Rowe founded, Ross Daley, who himself was a former Labor staffer in Queensland and professional lobbyist, was sacked for taking a $1 million payment for shifting $100 million of superannuation funds to his Mate's investment business (Dunlevy, 2009b).

But if you thought union control of Australia's super-annuation system was a cosy environment for a Game of Mates, the retail funds, which are run for profit and mostly owned by the major banks, have taken the Game up a notch. They have lobbied to wrest control from the unions over employee default funds in order to capture a share of the enormous flow of economic honey that is the superannuation system.

Retail funds typically underperform the industry funds because of their additional fees and the way they package costly extra services into member accounts, of which many account holders are unaware. The government regulator of finan-cial services, the Australia Prudential Regulation Authority (APRA) released research in 2012 showing that it was common for retail super funds to package insurance in their accounts from financially related parties, adding a high, and potentially unnecessary, cost to each superannuation account holder (Liu and Arnold, 2012). They found that these cushy insurance deals by super funds resulted in higher priced insurance, and much more complex insurance packages, costing members 73 per cent more for life insurance than other types of funds. This simple abuse of discretion over insurance in superannuation packages cost members of retail funds $15 million in 2012 alone. Retail funds are the experts at taking advantage of Sam being quite blind to the true nature of superannuation. They ensure fee structures are complex, and that many packaged products are included, like insurance and financial planning services, that are paid for whether they are used or not.[9]

Through the control of investment choices by these funds, and the ability to charge a range of fees to customers who have few choices, James now owns the largest buildings in the major cities, the headquarters of the super funds, and employs an army of lobbyists to avoid his spoils from being threatened. He employs former government ministers to argue for increases in the amount of income that workers have put in their super funds, and he commissions research papers explaining how workers would make bad choices if they were left to look after their own retirement savings, despite the evidence that the private savings declined when superannuation became compulsory, offsetting around a third of economic benefits of the scheme alone, meaning that Sam was doing quite well saving all by themself (Connolly and Kohler, 2004).[10]

In addition to all the hidden deals inside superannuation funds, the laws governing the tax treatment of super-annuation have been tilted in favour of the exceptionally wealthy, meaning James and his Mates. A wealthy and well-connected James can avoid paying the high marginal tax rate applicable to his income by funnelling income directly into a superannuation fund, allowing him to get a discount tax rate of 15 per cent instead of a much higher one if he takes the income in any other way. If James earns between $180,000 and $280,000 a year, he usually pays a marginal tax rate on income of 45 per cent, but generously, each dollar he instead diverts directly to super is taxed at just 15 per cent. These massive tax breaks, known in the economic lingo as 'tax expenditures', or 'tax concessions', benefit only the top end of town. For example, fewer than 2 per cent of earners have a gross income above $180,000 a year and benefit from the largest tax breaks. Research by the Australia Institute shows these tax arrangements, which were designed to keep the wealthy and well-connected Jameses happy, mostly flow to the top 20 per cent of income earners (Grudnoff, 2015).

Rules about the tax treatment of superannuation are a valuable grey gift able to be politically traded. When the federal Coalition gained power in 1996, Treasurer Peter Costello introduced a superannuation surcharge on high-income funds to combat the discrepancy in tax treatments between low- and high-income earners, which had been an election promise. Yet, after much intense lobbying from the industry, and in a time of relatively low political risk, it was scrapped in 2005, with an estimated loss of tax revenue of $2.5 billion over the following four-year federal budget projections. Instead, a cap on contributions to super made at a discounted tax rate was introduced. It initially cut off only a small number of the most egregious abuses of the super system, but was incrementally lowered to be $27,500 in 2022.

The superannuation system in Australia is thus a beautiful example of the Game of Mates. By legally mandating unions and bosses to decide on which funds to present to the workers in an industry, the government inadvertently created the opportunity for a grand trade between union bosses and industry employers, who combined to defraud the workers. By then allowing banks and for-profit funds to enter the system, the politicians introduced another cabal of Mates to join in the spoils. The effect has been to pervert the union movement, as well as the retirement system, for all Australians.

The union movement is now deeply handicapped by the trade in grey gifts available to its bosses via superannuation funds, because it greatly reduces the incentives of union bosses to fight for the rights and interests of their workers. On the contrary, union bosses now have every incentive to keep their members quiet and docile, which is one of the reasons Australia now has hardly any strikes by unions.

The union bosses also have strong incentives to band together with other unions in order to have bigger superannuation funds and combine their lobbying activities to protect their positions. Perhaps as a result of this, the union movement in Australia very quickly consolidated after the introduction of the superannuation scheme, and it corporatised in such a way that union bosses no longer come from the ranks of workers, but come straight from the ranks of professional union officials aligned to the Labor party. One reason for this 'professionalisation of unions' is simple: union members who have been workers might care too much about their members and cannot be trusted to do the right thing in the Game of Mates.

On top of all this, the tax rules have been designed to provide generous gifts to the very wealthiest, and bred a whole wasteful private industry of stock-pickers who have trillions in funds funnelled to them because of the compulsory nature of the system.

James in action

In an analysis of this very story of union power in the super-annuation system, Fletcher (2013) trawled through the annual reports of 74 industry or public sector funds and found that 31 per cent of directors, and over two-thirds of the 'independent' member representatives, were appointed by unions. In the bigger funds at the time, such as Australian Super, QSuper, First State Super, the Retail Employees Superannuation Trust (Rest Super), and Sunsuper, 92 per cent of the spots theoretically available for member representatives were union appointments with very few having investment and financial expertise.

Appointments to the boards of super funds receive director fees, and union members with many personal connections can obtain several lucrative posts at the same time. For example, Bernie Riordan, a former secretary of the New South Wales Electrical Trades Union (ETU) and a former president of the Australian Labor party in New South Wales, had previously been a director of Energy Industry Superannuation Scheme (EISS), as well as a director of two companies which EISS part owned:

FuturePlus Financial Services and Chifley Financial Services. A claim filed in the Federal Court in 2011 by the secretary of the Victorian branch of the ETU alleged that Mr Riordan had received over $1.8 million in fees since 1998 from sitting on the boards of these companies (Fletcher, 2013).

Another example is Bob Henricks, who was the Queensland secretary of the ETU for a number of years. Until 2016 he was the chair of, or on the board of, three separate funds in Queensland: Electricity Supply Industry Superannuation Fund (Qld), the Allied Unions Superannuation Trust (Queensland) and SPEC Super. Michael Williamson, the former Health Services Union boss in New South Wales, was reported in 2012 to earn $330,000 per year, in addition to $150,000 from his various superannuation board positions such as First State Super, hence collecting a neat half-a-million from his involvement in the Superannuation Game. He is one of the few Jameses in Australia whose trade in favours stepped over the line to downright fraud, and was caught. He served gaol time for 'ripping off the Health Services Union and then using friends and family to try to cover his tracks when the fraud squad began investigating' (McClymont, 2015).

The conflict of interest between union members and their superannuation fund has become apparent in court cases. For example, the Victorian branch of the Construction Forestry Mining Energy Union (CFMEU) applied pressure to the Construction and Building Unions Superannuation (CBUS) to help them in their dispute with the construction company Grocon. Against the union's wishes, CBUS went ahead and awarded Grocon a $430 million project contract, leading to the CFMEU seeking expressions of interest from other super-annuation funds to become the default fund for its members in apparent retaliation (Skulley, 2013). This is a good example of how players at the top of unions now increasingly behave like participants in a Game of Mates, seemingly putting their own feuds above the interests of workers and their retirements.

The role of unions in superannuation funds has also been a device for corporations to get lucrative contracts. The building company Austcorp, for instance, got a $30 million investment from the Meat Industry Employees Superannuation Fund. Unsurprisingly, Austcorp paid Wally Curran, secretary of the meat workers union and a long-serving director on the board of the fund, consultancy fees to make this deal happen. It's a classic case of a James at the top of an organisation getting private benefits for using the money under his discretionary control that belonged to others. A grey gift from a grey institution. Almost all of the $30 million investment was lost when Austcorp collapsed in 2009 (Fletcher, 2013).

In other cases, superannuation funds have been found to have corrupt senior union officers as directors, diverting funds for their own use—a more blatant, but also more risky, form of playing the Game. Craig Thomson, a former director of HESTA, a superannuation fund with $20 billion under management, was ordered to pay nearly half-a-million dollars in fines for misusing union funds after he was found guilty of breaking multiple Fair Work laws and using funds to pay for his 2007 federal parliamentary campaign as well as escort services (Akerman, 2016). On top of these roles, he was also a federal

Labor MP and the national secretary of the Health Services Union. In late 2021 he was arrested and charged with multiple counts of fraud for allegedly facilitating 130 fraudulent visa applications for a $2 million gain (Chung and Keoghan, 2021).

Behind the scenes, favour-trading is rife. By 2017 the effects of these otherwise invisible activities were felt by members, and a groundswell of community pressure led to the establishment of the Royal Commission into superannuation (and banking). Sam had finally had enough. Years of theft by James had led to a wave of public pressure to take back the grey gifts in a reform cycle that is quite typical of how over the long term James can be kept at bay.

Yet only one penalty came from that commission—a $57 million fine to NAB-related super funds for making false and misleading statements about fees being paid for which no service was supplied. On the upside, new rules proposed by the commission focused on better treatment of members, reducing costs and cleaning up the murky incentives in financial advice. But the favour-trading that occurs by the discretionary use of the massive balance sheets of super funds to finance certain projects above others is something that is fundamentally hard to police, even if the intention is there. Indeed, even getting the proposed member-focused rules enacted has been a battle against James, whose lawyers and lobbyists have earned their crust making sure the rules are written to suit them.

The costs of the Superannuation Game

How can we know how much James is stealing from us? In terms of reduced taxation for the wealthy Jameses and hence higher taxes for Sam, the answer can be found in the federal budget. The Treasury estimates that tax breaks for super-annuation in 2021–22 were worth $36 billion, or around, 7 per cent of the total federal tax revenue.[11] What is even more bizarre about the superannuation system is that one of its purposes is to take pressure off the government budget for future pensions by forcing people to save for retirement. However, modelling by the Treasury found that the cost of tax breaks given to the wealthi-est superannuation account holders far exceeds any savings on the cost of pensions from having a superannuation system by an enormous margin (Treasury, 2013).

If we take a big-picture perspective, the age pension system cost the budget $53 billion in 2021 while supporting the incomes of 2.6 million pensioners (Services Australia, 2021). This compares to the $36 billion cost of tax breaks to superannuation. Analysis by the Treasury (2021) shows that superannuation tax breaks will grow to exceed the total cost of the age pension in the early 2030s. The Game of Mates has led to the odd situation where suppos-edly in order to reduce the budget costs of the pension we have enacted a system that costs even more, while mainly offering tax breaks to the wealthy who needed no incentive to save in the first place. Stranger still is that the 'left' of politics, Australia's Labor party, driven by the fervent advocacy of Paul Keating, is arguing to increase compulsory superannuation contributions so that the country spends more on tax-advantaged private retirement funds than on public age pensions.

The present situation has come about from a whole suc-cession of grey gifts. Sometimes we can give a reasonably precise estimate of the value of a particular gift. The unwinding of the high-income earner surcharge on superannuation in 2005 under the John Howard government was a clear and direct result of James's lobbying actions, benefiting just the top 1 per cent of earners. And we know from the government's own budget estimate that this grey gift was worth $2.5 billion over just a four-year period (Wade, 2005).

The biggest costs, though, are the economic losses due to the overhead costs of Australian super funds, which are the highest in the world. There were at least 44,000 people working in the superannuation sector in 2020–21, an enormous number (Huey Yeoh, 2021). By comparison, the Department of Human Services, which manages all welfare payments in Australia, including Medicare and Centrelink, employed fewer than 27,000 staff (Services Australia, 2021). The group of 44,000 people is a massive diversion of human resources that could have been used more productively elsewhere in the economy.

To calculate the cost of the super system we simply compare Australian funds to some of the cheapest systems in other countries.

As you might expect, it is easy to find out what the overhead costs are of the best-run overseas funds, as they are mostly government agencies that have full transparency. The costs to Sam from having their retirement wealth tied up in privately run Australian super funds is much harder to ascertain, as these funds have many hidden fees and charges.[12]

Yet accountants and researchers have dug through the information available and looked at the discrepancy between the returns on the investments of super funds versus the amount they pay out, and have arrived at the basic finding that super-annuation funds in Australia on average have overhead costs equal to about 1 per cent of the stock of their investments each year. A report by the consultant Rice Warner, informing the government's Financial System Inquiry of 2014 thus concluded: 'fees . . . have fallen . . . from 1.40% in 2004 to 1.20% in 2013 . . . Total superannuation fees were about $16.9 billion in the 2013 financial year' (Rice Warner, 2014). That was an astonishing 1.2 per cent of gross domestic product (GDP) in fees for superannuation.[13]

This cost of 1.2 per cent on the stock of invested savings compares to an overhead of 0.1 per cent that the cheapest government funds, such as those run by Denmark or the Netherlands (OECD, 2011). On the $3.4 trillion of funds in superannuation accounts at the end of 2021, a 1.2% additional cost equates to $34 billion per year of unnecessary costs to Sam, an enormous sum.

You might think that the difference between 0.1 per cent and 1.2 per cent is not that high as both look to be rather low numbers; but one is twelve times larger than the other. What is easy to overlook is what this difference means over time for any individual looking to capitalise on the compound growth of their retirement savings over their working life. The 1.2 per cent overhead is charged every year until retirement. So Sam pays 1.2 per cent at age 25, another 1.2 per cent at age 26, another 1.2 per cent at age 27, and so forth till the age of 65. If you add up that cost every year, then the lifetime cost is closer to 27 per cent of your total potential superannuation balance.

Australia's superannuation system also has massive costs due to 'zombie' duplicate accounts that get created when people start new jobs that come tied to new superannuation funds. This means that people pay administration costs twice, and often end up paying for multiple unwanted and unnecessary insurance products that get bundled in by default. The Productivity Commission in 2019 found that

- A third of accounts (about 10 million) are unintended multiple accounts. These erode members' balances by $2.6 billion a year in unnecessary fees and insurance.
- Not all members get value out of insurance in super. Many see their retirement balances eroded—often by more than $50,000—by duplicate or unsuitable (even 'zombie') policies (Productivity Commission, 2019, p. 2)

To make these burdensome administration costs visible, the graph in Figure 2 shows you what happens to the superannuation wealth of the average person in Australia; the person who obtains the average weekly earnings from age fifteen to age 65. Of course, no person in reality fits this average, but the earnings profile (which goes from low to high in middle age, and then drops again after 50) is typical enough to make the point. To make sure we do not exaggerate, we use a cost of 1 per cent per year rather than 1.2 per cent, which is probably closer to where costs are today, and hence ignore much of the costs incurred over the past few decades.

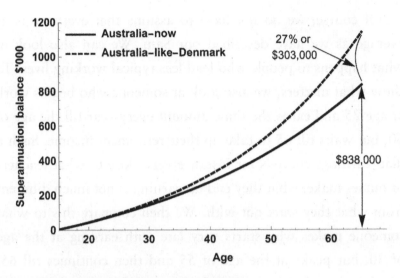

Figure 2: **Superannuation for Sam compared to Denmark**

The top line shows how superannuation accumulates by age if someone earned the average weekly 2016 full-time earnings in Australia of $1575, made a 12 per cent superannuation contribution each year (which is where Australian compulsory super amounts will be in 2025), and faced the overhead costs of Danish retirement savings funds, whilst making a usual long-run return on invested wealth of 4 per cent.

As you can see, such a person ends up with about $1.1 million in superannuation wealth at the age of 65. In contrast, the actual Australian ends up with $838,000 in superannuation, 27 per cent less than they would make in the Danish system (or put another way, 36 per cent more than the Australian system). James has gobbled up 27 per cent of the potential gains, effectively meaning that just in superannuation alone, Sam loses 27 per cent of their retirement savings due to James.

Of course, we do not have to assume that everyone is as average as we have described our Sam. We can also look at what happens to people who lead less typical working lives. To show what matters, we also look at someone who begins work at age 25 and earns the same amount every year till the age of 60, but waits till 65 to take up their retirement income. Such a 'flat' earnings curve is for instance very close to what teachers or nurses make: what they end up earning is not much different from what they start out with. We then compare this to what someone makes who starts very late with earning at the age of 30, but peaks at the age of 55 and then continues till 65, which is roughly what you see with people like medical specialists or lawyers; they start out making a little, but end up with large salaries that persist till a late age.

Obviously, the doctors end up with much higher superannuation balances than the nurses. But as you can see in Figure 3, there is also a difference in the proportion of their wealth eaten up by James: James wrangles only 15 per cent of the superannuation of the doctors, but 23 per cent of that of the nurses (and 27 per cent for our simple Sam example). The difference arises because the nurse has their savings tied up in the superannuation system longer than the doctor. And both have less taken away from them than Sam, the average Australian, who starts working earlier and hence pays a bigger proportion in fees.

Perversely, superannuation is designed to benefit most those who hold their savings the longest, yet with James in control, the system works best for those who have their money in the system for the least amount of time, because they avoid most of the

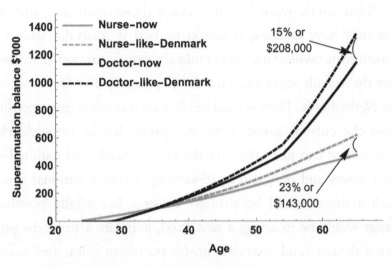

Figure 3: **Superannuation for nurse and doctor earnings profile**

rip-offs but get all the tax advantages. This means that any Sam who does not have high wage growth later in life suffers more from the Game of Mates in superannuation than others.

What should we do, and not do?

The economists at the Commonwealth Treasury and other government agencies have known about the rort in super-annuation for decades now and have done their best to thwart James's Game.[14] Yet in the face of this pressure, lobbyists and former politicians have successfully kept the Game going. This is quite understandable; the total amount of managed funds in superannuation is $3 trillion, bigger than the income in the whole economy. An additional 1 per cent fee on that balance is worth $30 billion per year, and you can buy a lot of political favours for that, as you can imagine.

What would work best to reclaim those funds for Sam? As you may have guessed, it would be best if Australia set up a government-owned and independently run institution that itself was the default super fund for the population, like Denmark or the Netherlands. There would be obvious transition issues getting from the current situation to this point, but in principle the government can just take over the private funds and nationalise their assets and obligations, re-forming it into a national fund. Such a move would be strongly resisted, but legally possible. Easier would be to set up a new fund, mandate it to be the pre-ferred default fund, mandate no-fee transition rules, and watch the private funds gradually empty of customers. The unfortunate reality in superannuation, as in other sectors, is that stopping James and his Mates after their Game has begun is much more difficult than creating a system that prevents it from forming in the first place, as occurred in the Netherlands and Denmark.

Tinkering with transparency rules and switching fees is a similarly hopeless endeavour, unless accompanied by a genuine alternative low-cost default fund. The reason James and his Mates get away with their Game is that workers have little incentive to read through hundreds of pages of fine print in the super-annuation rules. If you mandate total transparency, James and his Mates would simply subtly change the superannuation rules every year, send every worker thousands of pages of material in total transparency, safe in the knowledge that almost no one is going to read any of that information. Absolute transparency in a difficult-to-understand financial product like superannuation is just a licence for James and his Mates to continue as before.

Another option is to unwind the superannuation system entirely and let people take their money as income they can spend today instead. This would recoup many of the tax advantages that are going to the very top income earners via their super and increase disposable incomes of younger families when their spending needs are the highest.

Mandating a particular private default super fund is very much a second-best option. It requires being highly prescriptive about the contents and investments open to that default super fund, and it is furthermore highly politically volatile; any rules about default superannuation funds will be complex, offering a hidden environment for further grey gifts if any rules are revoked, amended or changed by the next vote in parliament.

Given that there is a war chest of $30 billion a year available to subvert the political process as soon as the population is not looking, we should not expect any lasting benefit from tinkering with the regulation. Mandatory super defaults or mandatory rules concerning the content and fees of super funds are likely to prove a very short-lived victory as James and his Mates will quickly work out how to circumvent those rules in conjunction with new political friends.

Some of the problems we have signalled in this chapter have been part of a large government review referred to as the Cooper review of 2010, which in particular honed in on the appointment system for who gets onto the boards of the superannuation funds.[15] In 2015 this led to a proposed bill that would require all funds to ensure they had an independent chairperson. The bill also proposed that independent directors make up at least one-third of the board membership, as well as requiring funds to disclose the interests of their directors (including positions on other boards that could cause conflicts). This bill was rejected by the Australian Senate (Collier, 2015), which shows how hard reform is in this area.

Even this failed reform was just a small one. Representation, in our opinion, is a very small aspect of the problem, well below issues like the ownership of those funds or the system for putting defaults in front of workers, along with the inherent problem of competition at all in a market so difficult for the consumer to understand. A bigger problem still is the generous tax treatment of superannuation funds.

In terms of favourable tax treatments, the obvious solution is to cut them back and allow the in-built progressiveness of the income tax system to function, treating all income equally prior to the choice of contributing to superannuation or not. In late 2016 there was a small win on this front, with some tightening of the comically complex superannuation rules that was on the whole progressive (i.e., was more generous to the less well off) and was expected to increase tax revenues from superannuation by $3 billion over the ensuing four years.

You may notice however, that this is only $750 million per year, which pales in comparison to the $36 billion the government itself reports as a loss from favourable tax treatment for high-income earners with the largest super funds. And of course, there was plenty of wailing and teeth-gnashing over just this small change.[16]

The only safe way to disrupt the Game is to take the value of the grey gifts totally off the table. This means truly making it impossible for union bosses or industry bosses to set up the superannuation funds for workers in their industry. Given the fact that the superannuation industry is now in the hands of James and his Mates, it would either require a wholesale nationalisation of the superannuation industry or else a government competitor that would be able to politically counterbalance the Game.

There are various things one should not do. It would for instance be a mistake to simply change the leadership of the current super funds, or to mandate oversight by new regulators or additional board members. This simply extends the scope for infiltration by James, who will very quickly be able to become that regulator and determine the appointment of new board members. The worst thing one can do is to leave it to current financial institutions and unions, since they have proven to be perfectly willing to team up to defraud the workers.

Another mistake is to expect any benefits from competition. There is already competition amongst many superannuation firms, including retail for-profit firms. But competition only happens if all funds have an equal opportunity to present their case to workers and compete with standardised products. That is not the case at all since there is a layer of unions and employers in between workers and the funds they get to choose from. Even without that layer, there is no guarantee that an incremental bit of extra competition would change things very much.

Genuine competition for a product like superannuation is extremely difficult. Funds cannot advertise their future returns, only their recent returns, which could have arisen by chance, so actual comparisons of which fund represents the best long-term investment are difficult. Advice from unions, employers and advisers will still carry weight because of this, and retail funds will still abuse this blindness to sneak in unnecessary fees, charges and packaged products.

It was no surprise to us then that the reforms to super in 2021 were primarily focused on promoting the semblance of competition. James knows how to create the appearance of major change without much change at all.

Called the 'Your Future, Your Super' regulations, these apply to the 70 per cent of superannuation assets held within the 160 or so large institutional funds (not the roughly 600,000 self-managed superannuation accounts). The upside of these reforms is that they should solve the issue of costs arising from account duplication by adopting a 'stapled' transferable fund set-up. This is a bit like transferable mobile phone numbers for which mobile phone companies are not allowed to charge. The new set-up supposedly avoids new funds being created whenever people start new jobs, a win for Sam that could be worth $3 billion a year.

The competition-promoting element of the 2021 rules was a 'name and shame' transparency initiative based on monitoring investment performance over the previous eight years. As we have noted, we think this will have little effect on actual choices of funds, as similar information is already available to super account holders who want to look for it. It is also rather easy to pretend to have had particular 'performance levels' in the past by playing around with the definitions of performance. James is rather good at such things.

Where the new rules might have power is that funds that fail to meet the benchmark return for two years in a row will have to notify members of this failure and will be unable to accept new members. This would then lead to further industry consolidation as the assets of underperforming funds are rolled into other funds, or as larger funds buy smaller ones that expect to fail the test. Indeed, such mergers have occurred in anticipation of these rules.

Yet, as one might imagine, these additional rules require new regulations that immediately become a new Game for James to play. The regulator overseeing the benchmark test is a prime target for James, so we solidly expect that regulator to be a James. Whether the benchmark test should be net of administration fees was hotly contested by James and his Mates controlling high-fee funds. They were ultimately only partially successful, with loopholes left in the regulations so that only the last year's administration fees are included, rather than each year of the eight-year assessment period. This leaves the door open for trickery when it comes to how and when fees are charged. Also, of course, James can have another go at nudging these regulations in future years.

In summary, after decades of James and his Mates raking in billions via the superannuation industry, the sheer scale of the theft created a small political window for some minor changes. The 2021 reforms have been promised to recoup about $3 billion per year out of $30 billion in administration fees for the Sams of the nation; potentially more if the reforms lead to mergers and the elimination of high-fee funds from the system.

The 2021 reforms are a small step. But remember, James is no fool. With $3 trillion of wealth tied up in the system, the Game will continue to be fiercely played. Genuine reformers need to pay close attention to whether the new rules work in practice as intended, and how James abuses their complexity to steal Sam's retirement savings in new ways. The very fact that minor reforms are all that decades of anti-corruption pressure was able to secure tells one the sector is still very much in the grips of the Game.

6
Mates

The first ingredient of the Game of Mates is the grey gift: a highly valuable, and mostly hidden, discretionary favour that James can give at no cost to himself—only at a cost to Sam.

The second ingredient for the Game of Mates, as you might have guessed, is a group of Mates. The ability to give a grey gift means nothing to James without his Mates. It is too easy for the public at large to see when politicians and government officials favour themselves directly. Cases of individual theft and fraud are relatively easy to uncover. It would be far too easy to combat this behaviour from a few 'bad eggs', who can be removed from their position of power. Such behaviour can easily be identified as corruption and be punished as such.

But with a group of loyal Mates who also involve themselves in making the rules and exercising discretion over who gets the grey gifts they control, James is able to conduct the Game with ease and out of sight. James need not favour himself directly.

Rather, James favours his Mates, who later return the favour to him and others in their 'club'. Together, James and his Mates create an informal group by trading direct or indirect reciprocal favours, which over time evolves into a social structure that bears a remarkable resemblance to a mafia.

Unlike the Mafia however, there is no need for conspiracy. The formation of informal groups who exchange favours amongst themselves is a natural human tendency. In some cases, these tendencies lead to the formation of cohesive social groups with common interests that provide benefits to both themselves and others outside the group; study groups, professional societies, resident associations, protest movements, interest groups, sports associations, and more. In other cases, the informal social groups that form impose massive costs on others. The groups that have access to the political and legal structures of society, and the valuable grey gifts within, are the ones to be wary of, as the power given to them by society at large means that when they exercise their discretion to promote internal cohesion and cooperation, it often comes at an enormous cost to outsiders.

James rules the roost in these types of groups, and the sad reality of this group dynamic is that James does not care how much it costs Sam to offer his Mate a favour. This has long been known. For example, Mançur Olson (1982) remarked that groups will impose external costs as they redistribute gains towards themselves that can 'exceed the amount redistributed by a huge multiple'. For James to give a grey gift worth $1 to his Mates he is happy to impose a cost on Sam of $10. This is why the Game of Mates is so costly, and why we focus so much on trying to understand the sheer magnitude of the economic costs; not only does James redistribute economic wealth away from Sam, he is an enormous drag on economic growth and overall prosperity.

In Figure 4 we can see three cartoon panels that help describe this 'groupish', rather than selfish, characteristic of the Game of Mates and distinguish it from both simple theft and bribery. In the top panel, we see how the politician or bureaucrat is able to directly steal from Sam for himself, for instance by pocketing tax receipts, or purchasing personal items with public money. This type of behaviour is relatively easy to combat, and one of the great accomplishments of modern Australia is just how difficult it is for those holding power, particularly in political office, to simply pocket the economic resources of the public for themselves.

The next panel shows how the politician can be directly bribed by others to give them the benefit of grey gifts. Here there is a direct exchange of money from James to the politician or bureaucrat, who himself passes money from the public to James. This type of straightforward kickback works well for one-off deals but is just one step removed from the plain old theft. In Australia, politicians have gone to gaol for this type of behaviour, as the law is designed to protect the public from it, and it does so with a fair degree of success.[17] But the incentive to try it on remains, as it is much quicker and more straightforward than fully committing to a long-run Game of Mates.

Watchdogs have commented on just how difficult it is to police this kind of kickback bribery in modern Australia. The

Figure 4: The social relations of theft, outright bribery, and the 'groupish' Game of Mates

New South Wales Independent Commission Against Corruption's Operation Spicer investigation found many cases of conflicted interests and financial deals amongst New South Wales property developers, though they seemed hesitant to call out the behaviour for what it is. The law still has a way to go in ridding the political class of outright bribery, but even so, this is a small part of the Game of Mates.

The bottom panel in Figure 4 captures how the Game of Mates is actually played. This more complex Game requires many players (we show three here for simplicity, though it can involve dozens, or hundreds), who simply offer grey gifts to each other without taking anything directly in return, with none of the many favours falling foul of laws that constrain direct theft and bribery. Sam's pockets need not be picked in a legally criminal sense, since the grey gifts are often within the scope of the law. Sam simply never gets the income, and never really sees that they are losing out from it. No one in the Game of Mates asks for direct trades, with the wealth stolen being shared through many repeated indirect favours. The Game is cronyism writ large.

Not only are politicians and those in power involved in such Games, but so too are technical staff, such as accountants, town planners, lawyers and others, who all benefit from loyalty to their powerful clients in their industry.

The grey gifts exchanged are also spaced out over time, avoiding the need for direct money exchanges. Grey gifts earn you credit amongst the group, who will repay you, directly or indirectly, later. This understanding helps to solve some of the puzzling aspects of political donations. Politicians give grey gifts worth thousands of times the value of the political donations. So why don't they hold out for more valuable donations from other potential recipients? Why sell themselves short? The reason is that there are other future favours still to come to them. Because James donates just $1 to receive thousands of dollars in economic gains, he is obliged by the norms of the Game to spend some of those spoils taken from Sam on his Mates amongst the group over time, and perhaps even directly on the politicians involved with the original decision. Favours given to political donors are simply long-term investments in the economic gains of the group.

The future gains for politicians who participate in the Game of Mates come in the form of cushy appointments to boards of directors, or as internal advisers to companies they have previously favoured, through fees for lobbying, and through future in-kind gifts. In-kind gifts can be things like accommodation at the holiday apartments owned by other Jameses, scholarships for their children's education, places for their children at universities, and more.[18]

The complexity of this favour-exchange Game makes it very different from simple bribery. Doing favours for people in the same group will inevitably mean not all favours are reciprocated. Sometimes a politician will get a favour and never be in a position for it to be returned. Sometimes James will get a favour from someone who has themselves not received a favour yet and might never get one in the future. This means that the number of favours done in a group is much higher than whatever we can estimate by looking at what any particular James has given or received.

The complexity and the inherent possibility of things 'going wrong' is one of the main reasons we know about this Game. Sometimes people in these groups feel they haven't gained their fair share and rat on the others in their group. This is often how large scandals get exposed; someone breaks rank.

It is not always the case that groups of Jameses form exclusively to play the Game of Mates. Often the groups that form around the valuable grey gifts on offer are those that previously formed for other reasons: through marriages, previous careers, school ties, and more. For example, former Queensland premier and Brisbane City Council mayor, Campbell Newman, married into a family of property developers. He failed to disclose these indirect property interests and was embroiled in allegations of corruption over favourable government decisions given to his father-in-law (McKenna, 2012). We can see that the Game of Mates will arise with established groups once you give some of them access to the valuable grey gifts.

The importance of reciprocity amongst a group also reveals the problem with revolving doors, which do not just operate at the political level but also at the lower levels in organisations that also have access to grey gifts, such as large monopolists and regulatory agencies. In town planning, the rotation of staff between the government departments assessing planning applications and private consultants who make applications for developers is common, even normal.

There are also banking regulators who have spent years working in the executive teams of the major banks. The authors can attest to repeated examples of staff at Queensland's independent regulator, the Queensland Competition Authority, rotating in and out of lobbyist organisations such as the Queensland Resources Council, who represent the very companies the agency is meant to regulate in the public interest. As one former banking insider said: 'Sometimes it is the politicians themselves, telling you to use their wife's consultancy, or a certain lobbyist to get a deal done, which is just a way of getting money to the politician. Sometimes it's the bureaucrats who have the power to sign off on your project, who want you to give them a job on $2 million a year after they've given you the deal' (Overington, 2016; quoting Bill Moss).

Often the revolving door is visible, with local developers seeking office after years in the local property development game. One example is Tom Tate, mayor of the Gold Coast and a former property developer.

The clubs that are formed know how to keep scrutiny at bay. When Queensland hired its first integrity commissioner in 2010 to focus on corruption and conflicts within the parliament, for instance, James and his Mates made sure the appointment would not stifle their Game. The Mates managed to make it a part-time appointment of a single individual with no staff, whose job was to advise on matters of integrity and accountability for Queensland elected politicians at all levels, their staff and senior public officials. Given the huge nature of the job, having a part-time individual with no resources do it, and even more strangely, with no legal avenue for making public the advice they give to politicians, is simply a form of window-dressing. It took a decade until the commissioner's role was resourced more fully.

The following story is indicative of how blatant the Game has become, with former prime minister Tony Abbott openly and directly inviting the mining industry to repay former resources minister Ian Macfarlane with a cushy appointment.

Tony Abbott gave us a peek behind the curtain yesterday, in his tribute to former resources minister Ian Macfarlane, a man so loyal to the Liberal Party that he tried—and failed—to defect to the Nats [National Party] late last year. Said Abbott: 'It was a magnificent achievement by the [member] for Groom in his time as minister . . . and I hope the sector will acknowledge and demonstrate their gratitude to him in his years of retirement from this place.'

Yes, Abbott is openly calling for the mining industry to repay the former minister's kindness with a cushy job, just as it did with Labor's Martin Ferguson. And it is the same way so many industries reward former pollies who did them a solid during their parliamentary careers. (Crikey, 2016)

Just months later, Macfarlane was repaid by the Queensland Resources Council lobby group who appointed him the new CEO (Corbett, 2016).

In 2019, former federal MP Christopher Pyne, who spent his years in parliament supporting South Australian special interests in defence contracting, even becoming the Minister for Defence Industry from 2016 to 2018, took a job as a defence consultant for multinational consultant firm EY just 18 months after leaving parliament (Iggulden, 2019). He also registered as a lobbyist for his co-owned company GC Advisory Pty Ltd, which lists a range of defence contractors amongst its 35 clients from many industries in Australia's Game of Mates, like media, property development and finance.[19]

To be clear: the Game is not a grand conspiracy. James and his Mates do not have monthly meetings where they conspire against Sam. The process of informal group formation arises over a long time as small favours are given, then reciprocated, before larger favours are given as well. It is human nature to want to reciprocate favours, and it feels good to do so. Many Jameses in the Game of Mates probably genuinely believe that, when they give their Mate a favour, it is the right thing to do, not only for their group, but for Sam and the country as a whole. The result is something that looks like a grand conspiracy to defraud the public, but in reality, the number of individuals in these groups who really know the nature of what they are doing is, we think, limited.

In terms of the groups involved in the Game of Mates across different industries in Australia, it is best to think of them as a clustering of smaller and larger groups, sometimes nested, some-times not. Consider the earlier example of superannuation. The insiders making the rules and running the show are a different, and more tight-knit, group from the much larger and diverse top few per cent of income earners who benefit from the grey gift of favourable tax rules. Yet in both cases the implicit desire to 'do right' by the group was present.

Lessons about the human tendency to form cooperative groups

To understand how group loyalty can arise quite quickly from favour exchanges, even amongst complete strangers and in the absence of formal agreements, we designed a computer-based experiment to see whether what we observe happening in the Game of Mates can be replicated in the lab. By doing so, we hoped to test which policy changes would work to combat the Game.

The experiment we designed contained the first two main ingredients of the Game of Mates: a valuable grey gift, which we simplified as a direct cash payment; and a chance to form a group through the ongoing trade in favours, as our design meant it was impossible to favour oneself.[20]

The heart of the experiment was to have four students play a game with each other from their own computer. The game had 25 rounds of choices over who would receive a grey gift. In each round one player was an 'allocator' who had to pick one of the other three players to be the 'recipient' that round. The person they picked would get the grey gift that round, which was worth $25 in our mock experiment currency (which would be converted to AUD so that players did have real money at stake in their decisions). The person who received the grey gift would be the allocator in the next round, able to then choose who to receive the next gift, and so on.

The catch was that there was a 'right' person to choose each round. Choosing them would generate the highest overall economic pay-off for the group. This was to ensure there was a cost to society (the four players in the experiment) if a group of two traded the grey gift back and forth each round. We implemented this 'cost to society' element by having a randomised 'productivity number' that was given to each of the three players able to be chosen to receive the grey gift in that round (randomly shuffled numbers 1, 2 and 3). In addition to the $25 grey gift the receiving player got, the productivity number would determine another pay-off that all players would get that round. If the allocator chose the person with the productivity number 3 that round, each player would get $3, in addition to the player receiving the grey gift getting $25 (so the receiving player gets $28 total, and the group of four together gets $37). If the allocator chose the person with productivity number 1, each player would get $1 that round, the receiver got $26, with the group altogether getting $29. If the allocator chooses the person with productivity number 1, because they want them to receive the grey gift, it costs the experimental society $8, or 22 per cent of their potential group earnings, compared to giving to the person with productivity number 3.

The picture in Figure 5 is what the allocator would see on their computer screen. As you can see, individuals were anonymous to each other as they were only known to each other as a coloured shape. In this example, the allocator was a pentagon. If the allocator chose the square in this round, then the square would get the $25 grey gift, and all four students would get one additional dollar, which is the productivity of the square player that round.

With economically rational players, what should happen is that the allocator chooses the person with the highest productivity

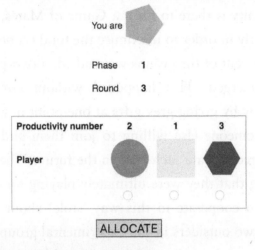

YOU ARE THE ALLOCATOR

Please choose who you would like to allocate the $25 payment to this round
by selecting the tick-box under their location, then click Allocate.

You are

Phase   1

Round   3

Productivity number	2	1	3
Player			

ALLOCATE

Figure 5: **Screenshot of experimental Game of Mates**

in that round (in this example, the hexagon). That maxim-
ises how much everyone gets. In the next round, the hexagon
(who has become the allocator) would then pick whoever was
the highest productivity player the next round, and so on. That
way, the total pie would be maximised. With a large number
of rounds, everyone's economic earnings are more or less equal
from this strategy, at around $230 of experimental currency.

Yet the game also allows for team formation. If two out
of the four team up and choose each other as the recipient of
the grey gift, no matter what their productivity number is in a
round, then they can keep the gift within their team. That hurts
the other two, who only earn $50 over the 25 rounds of the
game, but benefits the two that keep exchanging the gift, with

their group of two Mates earning $363 of experimental currency each. Hence this game allows us to see whether random students who do not know each other team up against others, because the opportunity is there to form a Game of Mates, or whether they play fairly in order to maximise the total economic pie.

In 84 per cent of the groups we studied, a two-player Game of Mates emerged. This happened without any communication. Simply by giving grey gifts at one point in time, players could find someone else willing to join them and repeatedly, and loyally, reciprocate such gifts in the future. The players did this knowing that they were ultimately playing for real money. Pairing up to cooperate in this way 'stole' about A$20 from each of the two outsiders in the experimental group, while also shrinking the total earnings of the group of four by about A$10 (or 11 per cent) over an hour playing the game. That's a loss for the experimental group as a whole. So just about everybody was tempted to be a James if they could. There were no differences in how participants played by gender, age or other demographic characteristic. The temptation to cooperate with your mates at any cost appears to be a deeply human one.

Even more interesting was what happened when we asked the participants about their choices in the experimental game afterwards. We asked players whether they were part of an alliance that traded favours in the game. Of those who were, which we could determine by our independent assessment of their choices recorded in the data, nearly half lied about it, covering their tracks to some degree. We also asked whether forming an alliance with others was a justifiable strategy. As you might have guessed, those who formed an alliance were far more likely to say it is a justifiable strategy than those who did not. In sum, if you are in the Game of Mates you are likely to conceal it from others and justify it as well, even in a low-stakes situation like our experiment. The lesson here is that if you thought you would be different from the Jameses we have seen across the Australian economy, most of you would be wrong.

Apart from the basic experiment described above, we also ran experiments that were similar but wherein some particular element was changed. In one such variation, we took away most of the value of the grey gift after an initial stage of 25 rounds, meaning there was only a tiny gift left to form an alliance over. We dropped the payment amount each round from $25 to $3 of experimental currency. Yet we found that even here, the Game of Mates persisted. Only when we started the experiments with grey gifts of little value could we deter a Game of Mates from forming.

This experimental result is completely in line with the way in which successful systems have been established in many economic sectors so far. The ACT planning system was established with the express intention of avoiding the creation of valuable grey gifts. The same happened when the Norwegian oil fields were established, and when Denmark's retirement savings system was created. It is much easier to create a system without valuable grey gifts so as to avoid the Game of Mates developing, than to take back the gifts and stop the Game once it has begun.

In the experiments we also implemented rotation systems to disrupt the in-group favour-trade amongst alliance pairs.

This means that the person given the gift in one period was not necessarily the decision maker in the following period and thus not necessarily in a position to return the favour. The idea here is that if people do not know when they might have discretion over a grey gift in the future, they will be less inclined to start forming alliances with Mates. Our rotation system was relatively unsuccessful overall, as it was not purely random each round, reflecting the imperfection in real-life rotation systems: those chosen last round were still more likely to be the allocator the next round, and that turned out to be enough to see a Game of Mates emerge. Like when we took away the value of the grey gifts, if alliances were already formed there was no increase in group cooperation when we suddenly started to rotate roles. Instead, those who had been left outside previous alliances and were now rotated into the allocator position simply began to form their own alliance with the other former outsider. The competition between the two alliances undermined any chance of the four-player experimental group cooperating altogether to maximise the overall group pay-off. Once an implicit alliance was formed, it remained surprisingly persistent even with our many tweaks to the experimental structure.

The problem of prior relationships is exactly what we see in the revolving door of staff from the regulated to the regulator: a process that supports the Game of Mates.

The puzzling thing is that rotation is often used in practice to combat the Game of Mates. We, for instance, randomly rotate people into juries in the court system, which has a great effect on ensuring the independence of jury decision making. A jury is truly chosen at random though, with no prior relationship to those they judge. What we learn from our experiment is the same: that rotation can only curtail the Game of Mates if those deciding on grey gifts have no prior relationships, and no ability to form new ones, as their decision is temporary. However, when someone deciding on a grey gift is rotated in to power and has already-formed alliances with the potential recipients of the gift, then rotation simply increases the ability of a Game of Mates to form as reciprocity is made easier.

Another way we tried to break down our experimental Game of Mates was to improve transparency. We started explicitly informing each player with a warning screen of the wrongdoing of others if it occurred in a round, including how much the decision cost them, and what the best decision for the group was. We also replaced the anonymous shapes with photographs of each player in the hope of eliciting more cooperative behaviour. Neither made any difference. While we may in the future do further experiments to fully understand why, the best story that fits the data so far is that such transparency can serve as a signal to other alliance players of their willingness to stick with the group, even with a loss of reputation amongst outsiders.

When we used photographs, for example, players who knew each other in real life almost immediately formed an alliance. This leads us to question the role of transparency as an anti-corruption measure. There is already a vast amount of transparency about who gives grey gifts to whom, and how much it costs (which we have used to write this book). So it is hard to see how a little bit more transparency is going to lead to any change on its own.

What can be done?

Our experiment shows that the Game of Mates is often truly one of 'accidental Mates', rather than between family members or easily identifiable communities. In particular, we are not looking at 'evil' versus 'good'—everyone will be tempted to play the Game given the opportunity. Instead, the Game is pervasive because the gains from playing it are so big, not because James is so evil.

Therefore, the counter-moves against the Game must be determined on the basic premise that Sam is being defrauded and being treated as second class, not that all Jameses are inherently bad people. We should be angry that we let it come this far as a society, not that James and his Mates have behaved exactly like most of us would have if we had had the opportunity.

The fact that the valuable grey gifts get swarmed over by groups makes it ineffective to add more complexity or more regulatory layers of the same kind as those already there. Increasing regulatory complexity in the same vein as before can be easily overcome by James and his Mates actively co-opting new players. What must be tackled is primarily the value of the grey gifts, not the individuals within group of Mates themselves. The easiest way to remove the value of grey gifts is to sell them or tax them. As we saw in our experiment, without the temptation of these windfall gains, there is little incentive to start a Game of Mates.

In the absence of pricing grey gifts, the next best alternative is to ensure decision makers are independent, and therefore focused on overall social outcomes, not outcomes for their Mates. We have seen that rotating people into the role of deciding who receives grey gifts will only be effective if the people appointed are extremely unlikely to have prior alliances. We suggest that there is a role for juries of random citizens to appoint the top decision makers in our public institutions, as the citizens who are accidentally in a jury are extremely unlikely to have any existing alliance with the particular Jameses operating in that sector. One can also think of panels of foreign experts in various industries to be contracted to temporarily run the process of developing new laws and regulations for their specialist industry. Both suggestions essentially randomise who is the key decision maker.

Randomisation works against the underlying process at the heart of the Game of Mates. First, the random draw from a large panel of either experts or citizens means that the local industry won't know in advance who to co-opt into their Game. Second, the short-term nature of such a role means that the local industry will have a limited opportunity to bring the experts or citizens into their Game. Third, in the case of international experts, the desire to protect their international reputation will counteract temptations to join local groups of Mates. While James will protest that international experts won't fully understand the local conditions of the industry, this is exactly the point—such an expert will be able to judge the arguments put forward by industry players on their technical merit alone.

We know perfectly well that a system of international experts is effective, because it is the exact system used almost universally to determine who referees international sporting matches.

The practice of random citizens appointing the top of a bureaucracy or of an independent regulatory agency has also been implemented successfully in the past. The city states of Venice and Florence used groups of randomly chosen citizens for centuries to determine who would lead those cities, which helped those cities elect reasonable leaders and avoid corruption. They and other major Italian cities in the late Middle Ages used elaborate systems of citizen juries, also called mini-publics.

Another idea in this 'randomisation' vein is cooling-off periods between any term in public office or the bureaucracy and the private sector. Cooling-off periods are, just like randomisation, meant to break relationships. Many jurisdictions in Australia have mandatory cooling-off periods, but with generous exemptions. Like we saw with Ian Macfarlane, a former MP rotating into the mining industry lobby group, and many others like him, the exemptions in the laws about cooling-off periods are so large as to invalidate them entirely.

Further focusing on independence of decision making, we can also think of using juries of citizens to directly make decisions, not merely appoint the top people at particular organisations. For important rule changes to major industries that affect the population broadly, like the regulations in superannuation, or mining, or planning, these juries could assess the merits of arguments put forward by stakeholders and interest groups, and ultimately make binding recommendations or decisions. They could decide on major appointments to head up government agencies. Why not simply adopt the very effective jury system we have in the courts more widely for crucial, and valuable, government decisions?

A good example of random juries used in deciding on politically contentious issues is electoral boundaries in California and some other US states. To avoid the inevitable gerrymandering that political parties engage in when it comes to redrawing political boundaries, it is juries of random citizens that do this. By all accounts, this is working very well (Kuyper and Wolkenstein, 2019).

Unfortunately, the very opposite of randomisation is happening when it comes to top appointments of regulatory commissions. In late 2021, Gina Cass-Gottlieb was appointed by federal Treasurer Josh Frydenberg to take over as chair of the ACCC, the anti-monopoly watchdog that enforces rules about the conduct of commercial dealings. Yet Cass-Gottlieb is also a director of the family trust of the powerful Murdoch media family, which has a strong vested interest in competition regulation that can work to favour its incumbent position and strangle new online media competitors (Keane, 2021). It is implausible that a random jury of any sort would have picked her for this role.

What would happen to the many groups of Mates that now rule Australia if, in the future, the honey pot of grey gifts could be taken off the table? Our overall view is that once the value of the grey gifts is gone, the groups of Mates that formed around them would simply disband. There is little danger of revenge from James once the honey pot is gone because there is no other reason for the group of Mates to remain cohesive. However, while we can minimise the value of grey gifts in many areas of the economy, the very nature of politics always leaves valuable decisions on the table. In these cases, randomisation of decisions and decision makers can ensure a Game of Mates struggles to develop.

7
The Great Mining Game

Mining has a long history in Australia, from the gold rushes of the 1850s to the 2010s boom in shale oil and gas. At its core, mining is about digging up a fixed stock of things already in the ground and selling it. One peculiar aspect of mining is that it does not really matter much to the wealth of the population when the stuff is dug up or how difficult it is to dig up, as anything left in the ground can simply be sold a generation later. Barring price changes and inflation, it is not all that important if mining is delayed.

The fact that mining is a fixed-resource industry makes the politics of mining exceptionally simple: do the mining companies manage to corner the wealth or does the general population get most of the wealth? It is simply them or us, and in the beginning, all the rights belong to us. In turn, this also makes James's Game very simple: can James usurp the rights to what is in the ground with minimal taxation, or does he have to share with Sam?

James of course understands these basics, which is why he has been trying to muddy the waters for decades, so as to have some chance of persuading Sam that his interests are the same as theirs. In fact, they are diametrically opposed. But James is rather clever, and he has managed to muddy the waters in ways you would never expect if you were not paying attention.

A simple, yet fundamental, part of James's Game is to be given licences for mining on the cheap, later sharing the spoils with befriended politicians, councillors and whomever else is important in the system granting mining rights. In this regard, James is playing the same Game as he did when it came to property development. He ingratiates himself with the right people, gets himself on reform commissions, runs for elections when he needs to be the politician himself, joins the right clubs, produces favourable economic analysis and publicity, and generally plays a classic Game of Mates.

James also cunningly gets the community to pay for many of his costs. To achieve this, he had to move with greater stealth, presenting things like railway lines to his mine as normal railway lines, and harbours that were only there to sell his products as harbours for everyone, even if no one else lived close by (Grudnoff, 2013). Generally, the less the population was paying attention, the more he could get away with transferring his production cost on to the community.

The trickier part for James was to get himself low taxes for his products, again sharing the spoils of low taxation with the Mates he teamed up with. Clever accounting helped him, such as by smoothing his profits over time and keeping profits under the radar entirely.

You might wonder how James could hide his profits. After all, it is hard to hide wagons full of minerals and, indeed, taxes on the actual stuff dug up from the ground are the most successful form of taxation in mining, being exceptionally hard to avoid. Profit taxes are easier to avoid though, particularly for large mining companies who can afford to hire the best tax experts in the country—experts who often know the tax system better than the tax authorities themselves.

One particular trick is what is known as transfer pricing. This involves a multinational company, like major miners BHP, Rio Tinto and Glencore, borrowing money from other arms of their international conglomerate at high interest rates and lending money to others at low interest rates. This squeezes down the profits on the books of the Australian subsidiary, which reduces their tax obligations in Australia. Of course, the profit does show up somewhere, so the companies direct the booked profits towards those countries with lowest tax, and increase them in other global jurisdictions with more favourable tax rates. This trick is played by most large multinationals, yet for Australia, the miners are some of the largest firms in the country.

Cunning, no? This is but one of the tricks played in Australia, and one which has allowed the mining industry to reduce its local accounting profits over the last twenty years despite enjoying the biggest mining boom in history.[21]

Of course, many of the tricks James uses in the mining Game were directly negotiated with politicians, like in the famous deal made in 2010 between mining companies and the then prime minister Julia Gillard. Desperate to have the mining industry stop the media attack ads against her Labor government, which was in the process of increasing taxation on the 'super-profits'[22] of the miners, her government was completely bamboozled by the expert negotiators and lobbyists of the mining industry. Not only did Gillard agree to various accounting tricks, but she also agreed to a system where the new federal government resources tax could be used to offset any increase in mining royalties that individual states may choose to enact. She effectively used the muscle of the federal government to cover the risk of royalty increases to the Jameses who owned and ran large projects in the major mining states.

James's trickery did not stop there. It can be seen in all areas of mining, ranging from preferential visa treatments for mining companies to exemptions from environmental restrictions.

Perhaps the worst form of trickery that James devised concerned mines that had stopped being productive and needed to be closed. Here, the problem James faced was that closing mines officially is an expensive thing to do, as mines invariably leave large voids, waste and environmental hazards behind, which cost billions to clean up. In the Latrobe Valley of Victoria, home to open-cut coalmines feeding massive electricity generation facilities, the government forced the mining companies to give them bonds to cover rehabilitation costs of the inevitable closure of mines in that region. You may think that is a good sign, but wait till you hear the whole story.

When asked to provide a bond, James would massively underestimate clean-up costs to ensure a small bond. In a review of remediation bonds in 2015 in the Latrobe Valley, French conglomerate ENGIE, which owns the Hazelwood open-cut mine and power station, argued that remediation costs would only be $73 million. When the time came to officially announce the mine closure less than two years later, the company admitted the total cost would be $743 million; $439 million for the mine, and $304 million for the power station (Asher, 2017). No doubt government contributions to these costs will be sought, and the Jameses at ENGIE are likely to be successful if they leverage the fear of lingering hazardous waste as a public health issue.

In Queensland, internal government reports suggest the public will have at least a $3.2 billion shortfall between costs of rehabilitation and bonds paid by miners. The misinformation spread by James about these costs is very clear to the experts in the industry.

The Queensland auditor-general's report estimated some 15,000 abandoned sites in that state alone would cost $1 billion to clean up. Long-time energy and finance analyst Tim Buckley reckons it could be ten to twenty times that (Seccombe, 2016).

Another trick is that James simply refuses to ever close down mines, even if they have been unproductive for decades. He simply employs a guy to go to the abandoned mine every day, inspect the site, and then move to another abandoned mine, allowing him to claim that they are all still operational (roughly speaking). As a result, many unused mines across the country have been officially open for decades, allowing James to avoid responsibility for the chemical waste slowly creeping into the ground water, poisoning the population and the environment.

A relatively new trick that gets James off the hook for cleaning up altogether is to allow James to sell off the mines' assets to anyone, together with the liabilities that those mines might represent: so-called 'phoenix activity'.

Where was the catch? Well, you see, James could now sell off the abandoned mines for token amounts, like $1, to empty shell companies that would hence own a derelict old mine as well as the obligation to clean it up if the mine was closed down or inspected. Those empty shell companies are simply allowed to go bankrupt, leaving the community with dirty abandoned mines costing hundreds of millions of dollars to clean up. This practice is already illegal, but difficult to enforce. In 2015 Queensland passed an additional law restricting the selling of mines with public liabilities. Unfortunately, there is very little political appetite to improve enforcement, despite the best efforts of many noble-minded public servants.

These tactics are very well known.[23] Yet the various levels of government involved in regulating the sector still find it advantageous to allow Sam to pay for the once-off profits of James and his Mates, by becoming a Mate themselves. Mining is thus another example of where James sits on all sides of the table—he is the person writing the laws pertaining to him, he is the person deciding on what mining rights he gets that others do not get, and he is a co-owner of the mining companies.

A recent example of miners getting the laws written for them is the Carmichael mine in the Galilee Basin in central Queensland, proposed by the Indian multinational firm Adani. The Queensland government listed the mine as 'critical infrastructure', which allowed it to bypass other laws that ensure proper assessments of the mine's impacts, and opens the door to additional government funding for ancillary parts of the project, like rail, ports and road upgrades.

Oh, and the Queensland government also gave Adani an exemption from new water licensing laws that are designed to reduce external impacts of exactly these types of mines on external ground water and river water. So favoured are the miners by Mates that, in 2017, Rockhampton mayor Margaret Strelow and Townsville mayor Jenny Hill agreed to contribute over $30 million to fund an airstrip at the proposed Adani mine on the expectation that fly-in fly-out workers would primarily be drawn from their cities (McCutcheon, 2017). All it took was a little wining and dining. James's Game is just that much easier when the rules are written for him and his facilities paid for by Sam.

With blatant trading of such valuable grey gifts, it might seem surprising that the general population is nowhere in sight when it comes to protesting these great giveaways. Perhaps it is because the Jameses in the mining Game are so cunning as to portray a public image that is grossly at odds with reality.

David Richardson and Richard Denniss from the Australia Institute conducted a public survey about perceptions of the relative importance of the mining industry to employment and economic activity. The public believes that about ten times more people are employed in mining than is in fact the case. They believe that the mining sector is about five times bigger than it is, and that Australians own more than three times as much of it

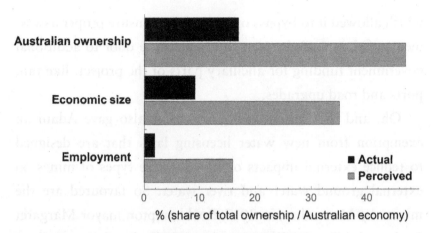

Figure 6: **Perception versus reality (Richardson and Denniss, 2011)**

(53%) than we actually do (17%), a misperception that is starkly shown in Figure 6.

Mining Mates

The Game of Mates in mining has become all too clear, and the public is now getting a glimpse behind the scenes.

For example, following her defeat in the 2016 federal election, Sophie Mirabella, a former member of parliament from Victoria, was hired by mining magnate and Liberal National Party (LNP) donor Gina Rinehart, as a Canberra-based lobbyist. In parliament, Mirabella's voting records were pro-mining, voting for a bill to allow unconventional gas mining in 2013, voting against environmental laws seeking to protect underground water from mining contamination, and voting against renewable energy investment and increased mining taxes. She got her reward.

The rotation of political staffers is so common that the *Sydney Morning Herald* created an interactive infographic on their website to keep track of them all. Journalist Anne Davies had plenty to say.

For instance, Martin Ferguson, the former Labor resources minister, became chairman of the advisory committee for the peak oil and gas industry association, the Australian Petroleum Production and Exploration Association, six months after leaving politics. He has been a fierce advocate of CSG [coal seam gas], arguing that NSW must forge ahead with development of CSG in order to achieve 'energy security for NSW.' His colleagues, Greg Combet, the former Gillard government minister for Climate change and Craig Emerson, her minister for Trade, waited a year before penning an opinion article in support of the CSG industry in the Australian Financial Review. They are both working as economic consultants to AGL and Santos, the two biggest players in CSG in NSW.

Former National Party leaders, John Anderson and Mark Vaile also moved into high profile roles in mining and CSG companies after politics. John Anderson became chairman of Eastern Star Gas, the company behind the Narrabri Gas project about two years after leaving politics. Mark Vaile became a director and then chairman of Whitehaven coal, the company behind one of the state's most controversial mines at Maules Creek. He is regularly seen in the corridors of Macquarie Street.

There are state and federal rules that impose cooling off periods for politicians and senior bureaucrats who move government to lobbying, but the act of lobbying is defined very narrowly to prevent only 'gun for hire' third party lobbying. This leaves politicians free to take jobs at industry associations and in business. In NSW minister [sic] must seek advice from the ethics adviser before taking private sector jobs. (Davies, 2015)

The story is the same in Queensland, where the local newspaper resorted to using elaborate diagrams to show the massive rotation of staff to the coal-seam gas industry, where the assessors become the assessed and vice versa (McCarthy, 2013).

The story is the same in Canberra, even amongst those not elected to the federal government. For instance, the former chief of staff for Bill Shorten (federal Labor party leader from 2013 to 2019) is Cameron Milner, who previously ran a professional lobbying company which advised Indian coal company Adani. We saw that company before, getting planning and water laws written in their favour just in 2016.[24] In Victoria, Geoff Walsh, former chief of staff to the then Victorian premier Steve Bracks, later became BHP's in-house lobbyist in 2007.

This list could go on, and it does go on for many pages online if you want to fully grasp the total normality of the entrenchment of James and his Mates in the mining industry.[25] And while each person's story is a rather mundane story in isolation, when looking at the overall patterns the real dynamics of the Game of Mates become all too apparent.

Costs to the community

There are various ways to get an idea about the costs of the Game of Mates in the mining sector. There have, for instance, been estimates of the costs of reparation for environmental damage done by mines that the communities will be required to pick up in later years. The Queensland government auditor suggests that in that state alone, the government has taken on a liability to rehabilitate 15,000 mine sites, at a cost of $1 billion.

In Victoria, the shortfall of rehabilitation costs of the three coalmines in the Latrobe Valley is estimated to be between $652 and $957 million. Prior to the detailed analysis in the Hazelwood fire inquiry, only $42 million in rehabilitation bonds was held by the government to cover these costs. That inquiry led to much larger bonds being sought from the miners to cover future rehabilitation costs. But as the latest revelations of ENGIE, owner of Hazelwood mine, make clear, the true costs are probably even higher than these estimates, which are already twenty times as large as the bonds held by government to cover clean-up costs if the miners dodge their obligations.

Some estimates of future government liabilities for mine rehabilitation across Australia are around $18 billion, which gives some indication of the ballpark gift to James from these favours alone (Barker, 2015).

In terms of the costs of public subsidies for roads, ports and rail for the direct benefit of the mining industry, estimates were of a similar magnitude of around $18 billion across the country during the six years prior to 2014 (Peel et al., 2014) though of course these estimates are disputed.

Figure 7: **The Mates make billions from mining while Sam pays for the clean-up**

When the Jameses of the mining industry lobbied to dilute the implementation of the resources super-profit tax (RSPT) in 2010, it cost us. The budget estimates were for $9 billion to be raised in 2013–14 from that tax alone. The Labor party was trying to implement best-practice mining taxation, yet James successfully convinced the population that his interests were their interests, despite the fact that the mining companies are majority owned by overseas shareholders (i.e., mining James is not even Australian). Ultimately the diluted RSPT was scrapped a few years later.

In Australia, we actually do have a super-profit tax on offshore petroleum that works reasonably well. The Petroleum

Resource Rent Tax (PRRT) raised $1.7 billion in 2013–14. The tax revenues were equal to 24 per cent of industry revenue in 2003–04, though they fell to around 5 per cent in 2013–14. Still, this tax has provided revenues of $1–2 billion per year for the past decade, with a tax of 40 per cent of super-profits on oil companies. So we know how to implement it and that it works, despite rising avoidance of this tax as well (Aston, 2015). Even Papua New Guinea has recently revamped its resource taxation to ensure that the public at large does not provide windfall gifts to their lucky Jameses who get exclusive rights to mine and log their natural endowment of resources (Pruaitch, 2016).

To give some idea of just how much money is at stake for the Jameses in the mining industry, consider that mining profit margins in 2009–10 were 24 per cent of revenues. That was $51 billion of profits in 2009–10, where about $20 billion in taxation would have been 'normal' if the industry was able to be as competitive as others, where 10 per cent profits margins are the norm. Because James, rather than Sam, has ownership stakes in these mines, he has a huge incentive to keep the Game going. Furthermore, as the Australia Institute noted: 'If these profits were distributed evenly across Australian households, the dividend cheque received by each household would come to more than $5000. But of course the ownership of Australian mining companies is far from evenly distributed across the Australian community, as already noted. Indeed, around 83 per cent of profits will in fact be sent offshore to the foreign owners of mining operations in Australia' (Richardson and Denniss, 2011).

Had Australia enacted the originally proposed RSPT, it would have collected around $200 billion over its first decade of implementation, or $20 billion per year (Richardson and Denniss, 2011). Obviously, these estimates are debatable, and may be at the top of the range of how much we could have grabbed for the community, but they are indicative of the enormous size of the opportunity we lost during the mining boom because James and his Mates played their Game.

The watered-down minerals resource rent tax (MRRT) that was briefly enacted did raise $300 million in that year, which is less than 2 per cent of what the projected gains were from the original proposed resource tax of 2010: just 1.5 per cent of the potential public revenues of the original RSPT. Even the failed super-profit tax does not give us a full idea of what we are forgoing. It merely shows what we tried to get but were thwarted in doing so.

Probably the best way to estimate the total cost of the Game of Mates in mining is to compare Australia's present situation with a country that has managed to capture the economic gains from natural resources for the general public.

Norway is the stand-out example here. Through their joint government ownership of oil and gas companies, and its special taxation on super-profits from oil and gas companies, they have earned public revenues of $543 billion in the past two decades, out of total revenues from all taxes and charges to the government from the sector (including normal corporate taxes and royalties) of $1014 billion.[26] The Norwegian system applies a 78 per cent marginal rate of taxation on profit to oil and gas companies, comprising a 25 per cent corporate rate and a 53 per cent special tax rate for the sector.

We can look at the profits of mining companies in Australia in recent decades to get a ballpark figure of the amount of revenues available had Australia adopted a tax stance similar to that of Norway.

Figure 8 shows just how much profit mining companies gained simply from the global market conditions for their products, with profit margins over 30 per cent for half the years since 2001–02, vastly exceeding profit margins in other parts of the economy. From the financial years 2004–05 to 2014–15, the industry had profits of $546 billion. Taking just the super-profits, above, say a 10 per cent margin, which is common in other industries, and taxing them at 48 per cent, the difference

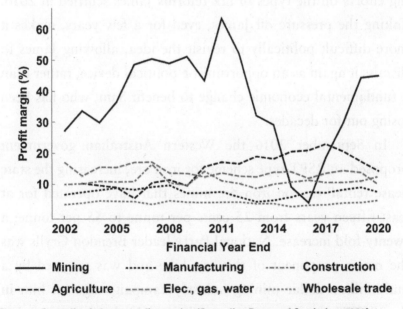

Figure 8: Australian industry profit margins (Australian Bureau of Statistics, 2021)

between Australia's corporate tax rate and the total Norwegian mining tax rate, provides a potential revenue of $171 billion over this decade, or $17 billion per year (around 1.1 per cent of GDP). In these years, around 20 per cent of the total revenue to the mining industry was a pure gift from the public. Add to this the estimated $36 billion in unfunded mine clean-up costs and subsidised infrastructure, and you have a ballpark estimate of what James has gained, and Sam has lost, because Australia's mining policy was far from best practice, thanks to the Game of Mates.

What can be done?

Several things can be done. First, the simplest thing is to copy the best practice of other countries such as Norway, by refocusing efforts on the types of tax reforms James scuttled in 2010. Taking the pressure off James, even for a few years, makes it more difficult politically to revisit the idea, allowing James to dismiss it again as an opportunistic political device, rather than a fundamental economic change to benefit Sam, who has been losing out for decades.

In September 2016 the Western Australian government proposed an RSPT-type scheme for iron ore, increasing the state 'lease rental' tax on iron ore mines that have operated for at least fifteen years from 25 cents per tonne to $5 per tonne: a twenty-fold increase. National Party leader Brendon Grylls was the major proponent of this tax hike and was targeted by a multimillion-dollar mining industry campaign against him in the 2017 Western Australia state election. He lost his seat at that election, with the Labor party taking government and scrapping the tax idea. This shows how difficult and dirty the politics of recouping mining windfalls can be, with James and his Mates ever vigilant.

Second, mining rights can be sold off in open auctions rather than given away. This is the same idea as in Chapter 2, where we proposed selling new property development rights by charging their market price to property developers (or close to it). Such a system was proposed by what is now the Productivity Commission back in 1991 (Industry Commission, 1991). However, in the face of harsh criticism from the industry, who put forward many of the same excuses they used to crush the RSPT in 2010, like the mysterious idea of 'sovereign risk' (by which they mean any change in legislation that negatively affects them), very little has been achieved to rectify the situation. Only perpetual stealing is deemed risk-free, apparently.

Saying it cannot be done in Australia or is impossible to put in practice is a similarly baseless excuse. Of course, the political timing must be right. We have already seen that such a system was enacted at the federal level for offshore oil, beginning in 1987. When a political window opens, taking back the value of political grey gifts given to the Jameses of the mining industry can be done. Indeed, such changes can even be put into practice in countries where grey corruption is even more prevalent, such as India, where the first auction of the right to mine gold took place in February 2016 in the central Indian state of Chhattisgarh (Drolia, 2016). The system has since expanded. In 2017, limestone deposits were auctioned with bids achieving twenty times the expected prices (Drolia, 2017). Nine coal deposits were auctioned in 2020, and sixteen iron ore and limestone deposits were up for auction in 2021.

Wins like this are rare, and usually changes go in favour of miners. In February 2016, for example, the Queensland government granted a 50 per cent concession of the promised expenditure for owners of exploration permits to protect them from bankruptcy during the mining downturn (Lynham, 2016). Add the generous grey gifts given to Adani mentioned earlier, and you see how the negatives swamp small positive changes.

A third option to reform mining is to increase the payment to the public in the form of state royalties for the resources, a very simple and efficient tax to increase that would share the mining gains more widely.

Similarly, the issue of environmental damage can also be quite easily solved by adopting best practice. By far the easiest way is to have mining firms pay up front, or in instalments, an amount equal to 100 per cent of the expected cost of cleaning up into a specific federal fund for clean-up activities. That ministry in charge would then clean up after mines become derelict. Alternatively, progressive rehabilitation requirements on miners can be enacted and enforced over the life of a mine, something that does happen on occasion.

While James is ruling the roost in the mining sector, having very effectively co-opted all the important politicians and bureaucrats, it is a sector where it is relatively easy to see how his Game can be disrupted, precisely because it is so separate from most of the rest of the economy. Only very few people work this sector;

mines cannot run away; the sector is dominated by a few large companies; the population as a whole has clear ultimate control of usage of the land, and it is able to revoke previous agreements. Disrupting the Game in mining is technically simple, but by no means politically easy.

Political leverage could come from exposing James's misdeeds in the mining industry. For instance, many mining companies will almost certainly have fallen short of environmental regulations and financial accounting rules. The US authorities have shown how you can exploit such misdeeds to force companies to agree to new laws—a political campaign urging the seizure of BP's assets was enough to force it into paying $81 billion in fines and reparations for the mess that was created by the Deepwater Horizon oil spill in 2010 in the Gulf of Mexico. Don't think for a moment that the Jameses at BP did not try their best to escape these obligations, but when the political pressure is there, James can be brought into line.

8
Burning Money

As is now clear, the Game of Mates is played by groups of Jameses informally exchanging grey gifts amongst themselves over time. We have seen how the Game is played by men and women alike (the Jamies?), with our experiments confirming how deep this human tendency is to form groups via reciprocating favours over time.

But now consider the problem that James faces when forming his group in a situation where there are many potential new Mates to team up with. While we have simplified our story by calling the representative person playing the Game of Mates James, the membership of these groups of Mates constantly changes. The world is not a static place.

Every potential James who has a grey gift at their disposal faces a dilemma when choosing who to favour: are they part of the group, or do they want to become part of it, by having the desire and ability to reciprocate? Will this person end up spoiling the fun by exposing the Game to the public?

For any group of Jameses to emerge, the problem of establishing loyalty within the group must be overcome. Because of the large social cost of the Game of Mates they cannot just send each other open signals of their intentions that could be read by everyone. That would give the Game away. But on the other hand, they often cannot entirely rely on existing groups of Mates that formed a long time ago. New circumstances require new Mates to join. And if promising potential partners come along who are powerful and have a lot to offer, they too would be welcome to join James's group if they can send a clear signal of their intention to cooperate.[27]

The third ingredient of the Game of Mates is therefore a suite of reliable signals that can be used by current and potential members of the group to prove their loyalty. As we will see, these signals come in the form of 'covert signalling' and 'burning money'. Without these signalling methods at their disposal, large informal groups of Mates could never form, and if they had formed for some other reason, they would soon die out.

Consider the initial signal from someone seeking out people who might form a future alliance, but where no informal group yet exists. What would you do in the circumstances?

The traditional method is to use covert signalling when approaching potential Mates. This involves feeling out a potentially important alliance partner to try to discern their truly held position on, and their economic interests in, a matter, all the while never directly revealing the real purpose of the discussion. The idea is that you indirectly plant the idea that the outcome that suits you is the outcome that suits them. You could imagine a brief conversation something like as follows between a representative of a company like Uber when it was trying to crack the Australian market, and a senior state government regulator, who have conveniently bumped into each other at the football.

US firm: Queensland is such an innovative state, don't you think?

Regulator: Yes it is. We try our best to foster innovation through our flexible regulations.

US firm: Yes. I've noticed that Queenslanders are embracing the sharing economy. We are expanding quite rapidly. So much so we are looking for a new head office to house all the good people we are bringing on board. Though they are hard to find.

Regulator: Well, let's just see what happens shall we? These are interesting times.

While we are by no means masters of the art of covert signalling, it should be clear from our rather amateur attempt above that the US firm's representative is feeling out the true personal views of the senior regulator without actually asking directly. For someone who is ignorant of the Game, they can dismiss it as generic boasting. But for someone whose interests may be aligned, who feels like there is too much regulation and who could be tempted into a job at the firm's new head office, the meaning would be quite different. For them it would be an indirect, informal invitation for cooperation. And that's how covert signalling works. With the right type of ambiguity, the message communicated will be different depending on who receives it.

Initial meetings of all sorts, in business and personal life, almost always contain covert signalling. It is the main way we discover the common personalities, abilities and preferred language of new acquaintances. But covert signalling also works to maintain cohesion in relatively large groups, like those in the Game of Mates. Government announcements that use bureaucratic and management speak often hide informal promises to help out Mates in particular industries, while lobby groups make similarly ambiguous public announcements in reverse, which work to tell the public that each side wants what's best for them, but tells the Mates that they will keep their promises.

After initial meetings containing a great deal of covert signalling to feel out potential Mates, it is a simple matter of seeking small favours, even unrelated to the primary purpose of the group, to establish trust and validate the relationship. Once the reciprocity of favour-trading becomes normalised, it is hard to stop.

As we have mentioned, most groups that form around valuable grey gifts arise somewhat by happenstance and evolve out of groups that had formed for earlier purposes: children meeting on a school playground; army recruits being assigned to the same platoon; young adults introduced to each other at work or in social clubs; and other situations that require close cooperation that will 'spill over' into other areas. To crack an established group, one of the first things potential new entrants do is to copy the language and behaviours of the group they want to enter. This can involve expressing support for the group's political beliefs and opinions about the economy, but also more social things like preferred music, hairstyle, clothes and table manners. Such copying behaviour is a type of covert signalling, which members of the group are able to interpret but that is meaningless for those outside the group.

As an example of shared beliefs as a signal, when we conducted our research on property development we interviewed several industry insiders. When the option of a betterment tax (i.e., selling new rezoning development rights, like what happens in the ACT) was mentioned, we had the response from one insider along the lines of 'You can't say that. As soon as you mention that word you have signalled you are an outsider and won't get access to politicians any more.' The language of the group is very important.

The next step is an introduction to a group member by a mutual friend. It works the same whether you are looking to establish business relationships, trying to infiltrate the Mafia, or joining a Game of Mates. This uses the trust of the mutual friendship as insurance while a small initial favour exchange is undertaken, which helps prove the cooperative intent of the new person.

People can do each other very small favours, ranging from speaking well of their friends in the media, to introducing their friends to other friends who have their own grey gifts on offer. Gradually the favours can start to include bigger things, from lucrative business contracts, to jobs and even potential marriage partners.

In modern Australia, this system of introductions has crystallised into a network of professional lobbyists, who capitalise on their own loyalty in the Game of Mates to take on paying clients, introduce them to other insiders, vouch for them and ultimately provide a mechanism for the group of Mates to evolve and grow over time.

Another way for an outsider to signal a willingness to enter the Game is to lavish gifts on insiders, what economists call 'burning money'. If a signal being given is costly, the willingness to incur that cost shows how serious the person is and makes the signal credible. If these gifts are themselves at the edge of the law, involving some personal risk, they also actively give particular insiders dirt on them to earn their trust. Maybe your company does some home renovations for a politician's family, but you make a point of not getting paid. Maybe you give them first dibs on buying off-the-plan apartments at a discounted price. These types of things may not be criminal, but certainly wouldn't be seen as totally above board by either party. The more reluctant the insiders, the bigger the gifts and the crimes would have to be.

Political donations are best understood as signals. A surprising reality is just how tiny political donations are in Australia. In Queensland, for example, total registered donations in the year prior to the 2020 state election were just $17 million, and for Australia as a whole, the amount was only $176 million in 2020–21 (Australian Electoral Commission, 2022; Electoral Commission Queensland, 2022). Considering that the state and federal governments decide on at least $400 billion of direct expenditures every year, and quite a bit more when we consider how politicians can affect current wealth levels by their power over grey gifts, the donations to political parties are tiny. This shows you that donations are not truly about bribing politicians, but are instead, we argue, about signalling a willingness to play the Game of Mates by burning money.

The distribution of political donations in Australia also supports this view. Over 60 per cent of the money from political donations comes from donors who give an equal amount to both the Australian Labor party and the Coalition parties. Why these balanced donations? Because the donors are not showing favouritism towards a party, an ideology, or a social or political belief. Rather, they are showing a willingness to pay to enter the group playing a long-run favour-exchange Game regardless of electoral outcomes. Because political donations are about signalling, newcomers to a political environment can find it advantageous to donate to help build a local reputation. This is part of the reason that Chinese property developers Yuhu Group, founded in 2012 and run by Huang Xiangmo, quickly became one of the largest political donors in New South Wales in 2013–14. During the wave of foreign activity in Australian property from 2012 to 2016, donations registers were dominated by new firms, particularly Chinese-owned, while many of the more entrenched Jameses donated far less, or even not at all (Uhlmann et al., 2016).

Regular donations by major corporations and wealthy individuals signal to both sides of politics that they are open for business and willing to exchange favours in the future. These donations signal that the organisation's 'credit' is good and that both sides of politics should focus their electoral campaigns on issues that don't threaten their cushy monopolies.

Whilst talking the talk and shuffling the walk engenders some initial trust, this is not enough to cement the relationships. After all, the grey gifts are worth billions and come at a huge expense to the public. Mates need to be able to trust each other with secrets that would be hugely economic and politically damaging if they got out. How do groups achieve this strong trust when there is always the danger that someone might grow a conscience, or simply out of anger dob in the other group members?

One trick is to ensure that the group members have dirt on each other. By knowing about the crimes and misdeeds of each other, their 'mutual dirt', they are bound together as a group. Mutual dirt gives each member the assurance that their interests will be looked after, which in turn gives each an incentive to do the others favours. Bound by mutual dirt, they all win by the favours they do each other because the dirt ensures the favours will be returned, and that there is no incentive for anyone to leave.

In his book *Codes of the Underworld: How criminals communicate,* sociologist Diego Gambetta describes elaborate and eccentric rituals of criminal gangs such as the Mafia and Yakuza. These rituals signal loyalty and filter out potential infiltration either by the authorities or by rival gangs. He notes that outside the classic signals of wearing gang colours, having heavy tattoos and using gang-specific language, one of the key ways to sustain coordination and identify willing insiders is to commit small crimes together to earn trust over time, building up a repository of information on each other 'available for mutual blackmailing' should either party renege on their implicit contract to be loyal to each other. As Gambetta explains in regards to Italian organised crime: 'This giant web of dyadic secret-sharing could sustain that pact of mutual support against the law which seems so strong among Italians, who display an uncanny predilection to privilege loyalty to their private friends over their public duties as law-abiding citizens' (Gambetta, 2009, p. 70).

When James and his Mates begin relying on the mutual dirt to sustain their cooperation, the Game of Mates has become a mafia in all but name. Would-be whistle-blowers have nothing to gain and everything to lose.

Of course, mutual dirt does not always work perfectly. Some people are just not good at keeping their mouths shut, and they will always become jealous about who is getting a bigger slice of the pie, even within a group of Mates. The ability to hold secrets and to accept that some get more than others is thus very much part of the initial 'sounding out' of potential group members. But in general, it works surprisingly well.

Sometimes dirt is one-sided and comes close to plain old extortion. In 2020 court proceedings it was alleged that in 2017 the then Ipswich mayor Paul Pisasale partook in the services of a prostitute 'JoJo' paid for by a Melbourne development company looking for favourable treatment for planning applications for their Ipswich projects (Walsh, 2020). What else was the alleged favour of the services of 'JoJo' but an attempt by a James of getting some dirt on someone influential? Unfortunately for the company, Pisasale was already under surveillance for many other offences. When arrested at the airport the following day he was carrying $50,000 in cash in his luggage. Though he had many florid excuses for the money and his behaviour, he ultimately pleaded guilty in court to no less than 28 fraud charges, two counts of sexual assault and official corruption. He was sentenced to seven years in gaol.

During the years he was partaking in corrupt activity, Pisasale was hugely popular with the public, receiving 83 per cent of the popular vote when he was last elected in 2016. This popularity provided cover from would-be whistle-blowers from within his party who sought to climb the ranks and dethrone him.

He also capitalised on the double-meaning and plausible deniability that covert signalling allows. When defending his actions in court after taking donations from a property developer he made the following comments.

> I championed the development.
> I had discussions with the planners . . . that was my job.
> I never asked the planners to do anything that was illegal.
> (Australian Broadcasting Corporation, 2021)

Ultimately the case against Pisasale only arose because those involved, both directly and indirectly, lacked sufficient cohesion. Whistle-blowers came forward with information from within the council, often at huge personal cost, to initiate the legal actions against him and ultimately unravel his Game.

There are other ways to access established groups. One easy way to access a group is to marry into it, or in some other direct way form a strong social tie with the existing members for a different purpose. This is a main reason for people to send their sons and daughters to the 'right' school, or university, or to join the 'right' social clubs. For instance, you might join the sporting clubs that the family of potentially useful politicians attend. Of course some potential Jameses use sexual relations to access the group, as happened with a town planner at Wollongong City Council, who slept with several local developers whose development applications she was assessing (Carty and Trenwith, 2008).

There are many historical examples to give of all these signalling methods. China, the world's oldest bureaucracy, provides perhaps the best lesson of how a system with a strong bureaucracy containing many grey gifts can be prone to gang formation, as well as how the counter-moves can be made.

In China, gift-giving amongst would-be conspirators who have no prior history with each other has turned into an art form, precisely because the bureaucracy has over the centuries effectively shut down less sophisticated forms of alliance formation, such as bribes or open theft.

What is now entirely normal in China, both within the bureaucracy and in the culture in general, is to give people the gifts one thinks they want without asking them what they want. Someone trying to get a favour from someone else does not ask them for a favour or even suggest any form of return payment (unless they already trust each other via mutual dirt). Rather, they try to second guess what an appropriate gift would be for the favour that is sought and then try to give it in a way that the receiver can plausibly deny even knowing about it. Such gifts are a mix of a covert signal (making a request without making it) and of burning money (showing credibility by incurring personal costs). Examples include the gifts given to family members or close friends of the person from whom they seek a favour. Later on, when the receiver of the gift is in the position to return the favour (such as a job, a contract, or a decision) the favour can indeed be returned, and all the while the two parties might truly have never met or talked about their exchange.

China also shows the next move that then ensues in this Game. The criminal gangs inside the Chinese bureaucracy, the 'Triads', operate like secret societies and have evolved over decades. A counter-move to combat these gangs was to have secret police infiltrate them, by having people pose for years as loyal members of these criminal gangs until the organisations were scoped. While Australia may still be in the Triad-development phase, unless some radical changes happen soon, our future might contain such counter-moves as having sophisticated investigators infiltrate the various groups of Mates.

In Australia we are edging closer to the level of sophistication in gift-giving and signalling that occurs in China. Partly because many of our major industries are monopolies, and are necessarily highly regulated, and partly because our wealth has grown substantially, discretionary political and bureaucratic power is growing to the level that was normal in China for centuries. Our culture is also becoming similar in terms of the regular abuse of this power.

As cultural experts in signalling, it is no surprise that the rise of Chinese company interests in Australia has seen a rise in signalling via donations, but also gift-based relationship-building by Chinese political interests. Former Australian trade minister Andrew Robb carved a niche consulting business to the now Chinese-owned Darwin Port for an $880,000 per year fee but was thwarted in 2019 by new rules about lobbying for foreign state interests. Bob Carr, briefly the foreign minister, was appointed the head of the Australia-China Relations Institute at the University of Technology Sydney in 2014. He spent that tenure fostering closer ties and relationship-building before leaving in 2019 amidst a wave of public concern. Amongst other events, the 2018 Victorian agreement to China's Belt and Road Initiative that would facilitate Chinese government–owned firms participating in major state projects triggered widespread concern and public realisation of the extent of the Game being played. In 2020 the federal government passed new laws that enabled it to veto such arrangements made by states.

An important implication of the way the Game is played is that individuals who are part of a group that does well out of the Game must be looked after by the others in the group no matter how badly they behave, because they will often have dirt on the others. They cannot be seen to be discarded. Good examples are the gifts given to those who have been found corrupt by courts and investigative agencies. The former vice-chancellor of the University of Queensland, Paul Greenfield, who was found to have unfairly secured a place for his daughter in the school of medicine (Kidd and Thompson, 2013) was rewarded for his participation in the Game after his retirement. As of August 2016, he was on the board of directors of the Great Barrier Reef Foundation, as well as the board of Healthy Waterways Ltd, and the Australian Academy of Technological Sciences and Engineering.

Similarly, Ian Church resigned as CEO of Tablelands Regional Council in controversial circumstances, after it was claimed he attempted to assault a union official—a claim he denied (Ison, 2015). He was rewarded within months with a new position as CEO of the Lockyer Valley Regional Council (Witsenhuysen, 2016). An almost identical example is that of the former CEO of Ipswich City Council, Carl Wulff, who in 2013 resigned under a cloud of misconduct, to pop up again in New South Wales as the CEO of Liverpool Council, again attracting controversy for his mismanagement of asbestos contamination in the region, leading to an apparent resignation that he revoked prior to public announcement (Dalzell and Hunjan, 2016; Tlozek, 2013). In 2019, Wulff pleaded guilty to official corruption and attempting to pervert the course of justice during his time at Ipswich council (Riga, 2019).

In late 2021 New South Wales premier Gladys Berejiklian resigned when an investigation began into allegations she directed grant money to a secret lover, but within a few months was offered a newly created lobbying job at communications firm Optus.

Incidentally, Orders of Australia honours crop up surprisingly often if you look at the people who we have found to be playing the property development game in Queensland. Perhaps these honours are a reward for years of service in the circle of

Figure 9: James gives his Mates awards to signal loyalty

favours between one James and the next. This tells you the involvement of the national parties as well, because it needs government and the central parts of a political party to organise Orders of Australia. Have a good look at the next list to spot James and his Mates racking up the prizes.[28]

To be clear: the third main ingredient in the Game of Mates is a way to signal a willingness to cooperate with other insiders. Because the Game is a cooperative raid on the economic wealth of the country, whistle-blowers are a huge risk, and elaborate ways to signal loyalty to the Game and protect the interests of all players are needed. This happens through covert and costly signals, including donations, attire and gifts, but also by accumulating 'mutual dirt' on each other, particularly on new players who are often tested on their willingness to cooperate by skirting the law.

The importance of signalling makes randomisation of people in top positions more important. When the top decision makers are appointed by people totally unknown to the Jameses in an area, such as by juries of random citizens, all the Jameses have to be extra careful about their signals to each other and particularly to the new top decision makers. Moreover, their investments into previous networks of dirt and favours are made a lot less lucrative if top positions suddenly get determined by people outside their circles. So even if citizen juries will now and then appoint incompetents to top positions, those incompetents will still disrupt the Game of Mates for the simple reason that they are not already part of the Game and might just have a conscience.

9
The Great Banking Game

Australia's biggest private companies are its banks. The four major banks have near complete control over the market for mortgages and loans to small businesses. At the end of 2021, the 'big four' made up roughly 70 per cent of the Australian mortgage and lending market. Compared to foreign banks, they make spectacular profits each year, with the big four booking $39 billion of before-tax profits in 2021, which is about 2 per cent of GDP. With a stable after-tax rate of return on equity of 10 to 15 per cent, banking is one of the most lucrative businesses in Australia.

How have James and his Mates cooked the banking game? Like we have seen in mining and property, James plays on both sides of the fence in banking: former bankers are amongst the executive ranks at the industry regulator, APRA; bank managers were instrumental in creating key banking regulation; major investors and businesses have direct input on monetary policy via their official representatives on the board of the Reserve Bank of Australia (RBA); and of course banks are major donors who regularly contribute to both of the major political parties.

In 2017, two former state premiers, Anna Bligh and Mike Baird, joined the banking Game as the threat of a national inquiry into bank lending practices gained force. Bligh became CEO of the Australian Banking Association lobby group, and Baird became the Chief Customer Officer at NAB for three years. Former New South Wales premier Gladys Berejiklian was a Commonwealth Bank executive before moving into politics, while Arthur Sinodinos, the chief of staff for former prime minister John Howard for a decade up until 2007, left politics to work in banking, first with Goldman Sachs and then with National Australia Bank.

Further down the corporate ladder there is evidence of a revolving door of cushy grey gift appointments that is symptomatic of a Game of Mates, as a Fairfax investigation in 2015 uncovered.

> Jeff Millard, the man managing supervision of 'specialised institutions'—insurers, according to his LinkedIn profile—came straight from Deloitte. Scott McIsaac went from being Operational Risk Manager at Commonwealth Bank to being Operational Risk Specialist at APRA. He declined to comment for this article. Michael Saadat, a senior executive leader at ASIC overseeing deposit-takers, was previously head of compliance at the local branch of Citibank. They all declined to comment for this article. (Mannix, 2015)

More to the point, James has been playing the banking Game for centuries and knows the two main ways government can be co-opted to earn him the big bucks. First, James can seek favourable regulation that kills off the competition. Second, James can try to get direct control over money creation granted to him. James has achieved both in Australia, but in Australia James primarily makes money off the first, citing as 'validation' the dangers of the havoc he could cause because of the second issue (the money creation). Sounds like a form of blackmail, no?

In Australia, killing off competition for banking has not always been easy for James. In the 1970s and 1980s (and earlier) for instance, there was a state competitor bank, the Commonwealth Bank of Australia, which competed with other banks and building societies to offer cheap loans and mortgages. James had to work hard to ensure that the media was flooded with stories about how ineffective this state bank was and how much better it would be once privatised. This indeed happened (under the Keating government in 1991) and James has been doing great business with the Commonwealth Bank (CBA) ever since, ensuring sky-high mortgage and business loan interest rate margins, frustrating truly competitive businesses that rely on efficient banking services.

There used to be smaller banks and building societies offering lower mortgage rates, particularly before the Global Financial Crisis of 2008, but many have simply been bought by the big four in Australia. James has been very effective at killing off the competition by taking over the competition.

Independent mortgage brokers that sprang up in the 1990s did add a new degree of competition amongst banks. But even in this sector consolidation has gone on unchecked. In 2008 mortgage broker Wizard was bought by another broker Aussie, who was then in 2012 partially bought by Australia's largest bank, the CBA. By 2020 CBA had acquired 100 per cent of Aussie. It then immediately merged it with a new online home loan platform Lendi, but in the process sold partial ownership stakes to ANZ and Macquarie Group, two other banks it is meant to compete with (Fernyhough, 2020). The fact that such deals proceed untouched and that major banks have not been broken up by government shows how in this Game the regulators are on his side.

James capitalises on his government-sanctioned monopoly in banking to make preposterously high profits in two ways. He either overcharges borrowers with higher interest rates, or cheats depositors with lower interest rates, and charges them both exorbitant fees for the pleasure. It is not clear which of these two ills is worse for the economy but in an ideal system James would not have either option.

In his dealings with bank customers, James uses many of the tricks we saw earlier in superannuation. His general rule has been to offer a low price up front and hide all the additional costs in later fees and charges that are hidden in the fine print, as well as high costs for switching to other banks. Hence you will find few up-front fees at banks, but lots of surprise fees that come late when you try moving accounts or mortgages, and enormous penalties for missing payments or doing anything not exactly in line with the advertised product. It is during those moments when your life is in flux and you step out of line a little that James fleeces you.

We have evidence of some of the ways Australian banks explicitly rob their customers with fees and charges. The CBA, National Australia Bank, ANZ, Westpac and AMP were all playing the same game of gouging customers with hidden fees for financial advice that was never given. Collectively they charged over 200,000 customers upwards of $178 million, which has since been discovered by the corporate regulator, ASIC, which has ordered the money to be refunded with interest (Letts, 2016).

It is not the case that James has had it all his own way in Australian banking. Many banking reforms have been proposed and some of these have been enacted. Lower switching fees for new mortgages and transparency in transaction costs have been mandated, whilst price coordination between banks is out-lawed.[29] Recent wins have been small, but there have been some.

For example, in 2017 the then prime minister, Malcolm Turnbull, pushed for a new tax on banks that reflected the value of their implicit government guarantees. The United Kingdom introduced a similar bank levy in 2011, just a few years after the Global Financial Crisis in which many government bank guaran-tees were enacted. While James did his best to ensure Australia's bank levy failed, the wave of public anger at the misdeeds of banks, that also led to the Royal Commission later that year, meant that it did ultimately pass. The Major Bank Levy has raised a little over $1.5 billion per year since, but is treated as a tax-deductible expense, so the net effect is lower still (Australian Parliament, 2020). Compared to the $39 billion in bank profits, this was a relatively small win for Sam.

Later in 2017 the Hayne Royal Commission was created to investigate misconduct in the banking and financial services sector, including superannuation. This was the biggest investigation into the financial sector in decades and the findings were brutal. The fallout was a relatively modest win for Sam.

Major banks where misconduct had been identified began compensating customers for previous scams, with up to $10 billion likely to be eventually repaid. Banks got new obligations to act in the interest of customers, which in some cases means automatically shifting customers to low-fee accounts when these alternatives are available, though this does not apply to mortgages—which is important, because mortgages are the biggest money-spinner. The changes to mortgages have been in the area of owner-occupier mortgages which have seen much lower interest rates than investor mortgages in the period 2018–21.

Against a player like James though, the changes have not mattered much, particularly not the regulations against coordination with other bankers. James doesn't need to pick up the phone with his Mates in the other banks to ensure he and his Mates all set world-leading interest rate margins on mortgages. His price coordination comes from a long-run Game with many employees rotating from one bank to another. James does not tell his friends anything, for they simply switch places every so often and ensure the systems that determine the pricing are the same in all the banks. An implicit and entrenched Game like this cannot be broken with transparency.

James has another trick up his sleeve; he can create money. While each major bank individually can only create a limited amount of money without proper collateral before it would be noticed, together the major banks can create vast amounts of money because what they indirectly lend each other counts as collateral. So together they can print huge sums of money and direct these new funds to benefit James and his Mates.

'Create money, really?' I hear you ask. Sounds like voodoo you might think. Part of some old defunct economic story? Not at all.

In Australia, and every modern country with its own currency and banking system, most new money is created by privately owned commercial banks. Money is created by banks adding numbers to deposit accounts (a 'liability') in exchange for a loan (an 'asset'), which is a promise to pay back, and usually comes with a claim over property or other assets offered by the borrower as collateral. The money created in deposit accounts can be used to buy things and converted to physical cash if needed. It is real money. The only constraint on the rate at which new money is created by any one bank is the control of the central bank over each bank's net account balances in relation to the other banks in the system (the RBA, like other countries' central banks, acts as the bankers' bank).

The fact that payments between banks must occur via their accounts at the central bank also limits the way in which banks can compete. It is extremely difficult for a small bank to grow faster than other banks by offering better and cheaper mortgages. This is because the money the small bank creates for new mortgages gets immediately spent by its borrowers at other banks, and therefore requires the originating small bank to pay the big banks from its central bank account (called an Exchange Settlement Account). This improves the big banks' financial position, not its own. This is why small banks and new international banks are always advertising their savings accounts to customers to attract payments to them via central bank accounts of other banks.

As you might have guessed, there is an obvious way for James to help himself to money in the banking system, although it rarely happens so blatantly. James can lend new money to his Mates, who in turn lend to him, under favourable conditions, buying up everything that can be bought. In principle, the entire value of the deposits at banks can thus be robbed, with James and his Mates using their new deposits to buy up assets across the economy. As long as deposits in their banks are trusted and accepted by the deposit holders, such activities could persist. Such blatant abuse is rare, but does happen occasionally. As we saw earlier, banks played a role in some PPP transport projects by lending new money to the unviable projects so that James and his Mates need not put any of their own money at risk.

There have been times when money was created by governments, and it is one of the policy options to do so again. Ideally, that money creation would be 'neutral', in the sense that money would only be used for trading and new investment, with no one being advantaged by the money creation. This transaction function of money is what economists call a public good; its value lies in allowing more people to specialise in what they are good at by making trade easy. It also means that the amount of money needs to expand over time as new real investment is undertaken that expands the total production and trade in the economy. From the 1920s to the 1950s, the Commonwealth Bank was both a publicly owned retail bank, creating money held in bank accounts that circulated in the economy, as well as the central bank of the country, issuing the coins and notes. Private banks hated the existence of the Commonwealth Bank state competitor, so they managed to get rid of it as a true competitor. It is now part of the club.

As an example of the rewards on offer from the ability of bankers to print money, including to some degree their own salaries, the CBA paid $44.8 million to its twelve executives in 2015–16, with CEO Ian Narev making half of that (CBA, 2016). That's about $60,000 of gains to Narev each and every day of the year, or $2500 an hour for every hour of every day. He made more in his sleep each night than the typical full-time worker made in three months. By 2021, the CBA executives had tightened their belts; the ten executives in that year got only a measly $33 million between them.

There is also Mike Smith, former ANZ CEO who was paid $88 million over his eight years in the job, a period that was characterised by a failed tilt at Asian markets and under-performance (Patrick, 2016). Like many others, Smith joined one of the major accounting and advisory firms as an 'ambassador' after his reign at ANZ (Keen, 2016).

There is no need for banking James to be blatantly criminal. He can rob depositors slowly, yet equally effectively. Because depositors will all lose if all banks collapse, governments fearing a general economic collapse will implicitly guarantee James's banks and rescue the banks in case the bad loans pile up too much, rewarding James for making bad loans. This provides an avenue for James and his Mates to create 'bad loans' for each other: loans that are unlikely to be paid back, that are big enough to risk the banks getting into trouble and yet that are small enough and complicated enough to get away with individually. They put nothing at risk because the survival of the banks is guaranteed by the public. Such actions were a major part of the US financial crisis, where banks had made new high-risk loans to real estate developers and buyers. One of the ways the US banks covered it up was to ensure the fine print to the high-risk loans ran in the tens of thousands of pages, a sure-fire way to make sure no one else knows what one is really doing. In Australia, we have yet to see if the bad loan game is played as much as it was in the United States and in Europe, but the essential elements are there.[30]

James also capitalises on complex regulatory schemes to legally protect his banking cartel. In 2016 the CBA, National Australia Bank, Westpac and Bendigo Bank brought a case to the ACCC seeking access to Apple's iPhone chip, which is the part of the phone hardware that securely processes Apple's own digital payment system, ApplePay. A successful case would have legally entitled the banks to act as a cartel to prevent competition from Apple, and quite possibly any new digital payments providers in the future. Though the banks ultimately lost this case, the effect of merely bringing the case delayed the adoption of new payments technology, increasing bank profits. Each month of delay is worth hundreds of millions, against which the legal fees are peanuts. While delaying ApplePay is small fry in the grand scheme of James's Game in banking, it serves to illustrate how James tries to twist laws to his advantage.

But there is a lesson here too about how to break the cooperative behaviour of James and his Mates. You see, Apple had already negotiated with ANZ and American Express to partner with its payments system before the legal case by the other banks had started. Apple tempted a single James to renege on his loyalty to the Game by offering him a juicy deal to do so. This had the effect of reducing the power of the banks to negotiate as a group, and undermining the legal arguments able to be made to the ACCC by the other banks, who foolishly missed out on being the first to jump ship. The strategy used here, and one that can often be used to break a Game of Mates, is to divide the group: foster an internal conflict amongst James and his Mates, and their joint power, which comes from their loyalty to the Game, is greatly diminished.

The reach of James in banking is a global one. If we look to the United States, we see that they too have a problem with James in their banking system. Author and political commentator Thomas Frank explained in 2016 how the Podesta email leak revealed behaviour of banking Mates in their political system, which is exactly as we describe.

Then there is the apparent nepotism, the dozens if not hundreds of mundane emails in which petitioners for this or that plum Washington job or high-profile academic appointment politely appeal to Podesta—the ward-heeler of the meritocratic elite—for a solicitous word whispered in the ear of a powerful crony. This genre of Podesta email, in which people try to arrange jobs for themselves or their kids, points us toward the most fundamental thing we know about the people at the top of this class: their loyalty to one another and the way it overrides everything else. Of course Hillary Clinton staffed her state department with investment bankers and then did speaking engagements for investment banks as soon as she was done at the state department. Of course she appears to think that any kind of bank reform should 'come from the industry itself'. And of course no elite bankers were ever prosecuted by the Obama administration. Read these emails and you understand, with a start, that the people at the top tier of American life all know each other. They are all engaged in promoting one another's careers, constantly . . . Yes, it's all supposed to be a meritocracy. But if you aren't part of this happy, prosperous in-group—if you don't have John Podesta's email address—you're out. (Frank, 2016)

When the stakes are as high as they are in US banking, the Game is even more clinically played than in Australia's relatively low-stakes banking system.

How much does the Game cost us?

One way to count the costs of our current banking system is to compare the profit margin on loans, such as for mortgages or businesses, with the profit margin of banks in more competitive systems. Essentially, this calculation provides the size of the gains that James gets for keeping competition at bay through his Game of Mates.

Let us look at mortgage interest rates. Mortgages are the single biggest earner for banks in Australia, with total private mortgages totalling about $2 trillion, which is roughly the same as the size of the total value of goods and services produced annually across the whole economy. As usual, we compare Australia with what is possible elsewhere in the world, in this case Canada. The Canadian government has an independent body, the Canada Mortgage and Housing Corporation (CMHC), that has grown and evolved since 1946 from a national post-war housing construction and veteran housing institution to a world-leading regulator of mortgage markets. It sells cheap mortgage guarantees to banks for a certain percentage of the value of the mortgage, which reduces profits on insurance able to be made in the private banking sector. The CHMC also provides a public scheme to purchase securitised mortgages from banks and other financial institutions through the Canada Mortgage Bonds (CMBs) program, which effectively removes a layer from the profits on mortgages that would usually go to banks and returns them to the government. These guarantees have the effect of keeping mortgage interest rates lower by diverting a chunk of potential bank profits to the government, or to borrowers.

In Canada, the difference between the interest rates that banks themselves pay on their own borrowings, and the mortgage interest rates (known as the 'spread'), has been around 3 per cent in recent decades. Prior to the most recent monetary policy cycle, which dropped interest rates close to zero, the standard variable interest rate on mortgages in Canada was around 3.75 per cent while their central bank rate was about 0.75 per cent, giving a 3 per cent premium. In Australia, the variable rate on mortgages was about 5.5 per cent, while the central bank interest rate charged to commercial banks is 1.5 per cent, a 4 per cent premium. Using World Bank standardised data, the interest rate premium Australians have paid for their mortgages was 1.3 percentage points higher than Canada, on average, over the first two decades of the twenty-first century.

As the rule of thumb, mortgages in Australia have historically been 1 percentage point more expensive per year than they could be. Although it doesn't sound much, it means that if you have a 3 per cent mortgage rate, you are actually paying 50 per cent more than you need to (because 3 is 50 per cent bigger than 2). If you had a 5 per cent mortgage, you would be paying 25 per cent more. Whereas in Canada the government makes a modest profit on effectively giving out mortgages for a low price, in Australia the private sector banks make huge profits by keeping mortgage interest rates high through implicit cartel behaviour. As you might already have calculated, 1 per cent on a total mortgage stock of $2 trillion is $20 billion per year in extra profits on mortgages. As we mentioned at the start of this chapter, in 2021 the banks made around $39 billion in pre-tax profits, so we are suggesting that around half of this is the result of James's ability to keep out competition or effective regulation from Australian banking.

Though monetary policy decisions worldwide resulted in collapsing interest rates in the late 2010s, and especially during 2020, the relative differences in interest rate margins remain, and hence so do the relative costs to Sam. When prevailing interest rates are lower, smaller differences have bigger effects, and when interest rates normalise, these differences will matter for years to come.

For the typical Sam, small amounts like the difference between 5 per cent and 6 per cent might not seem like much, but mortgages last far longer than a year. As we saw with super-annuation, small additional costs on large balances in long-term investments truly matter over time.

How much more do Australians then pay for mortgages in their lifetime than they need to? We calculated the answer to this with a hypothetical loan of $100,000 where relevant con-ditions are what they have roughly been the last two decades.[31] What we compare is the total value of the repayment on the loans, made up of the accumulated yearly payments.

The dashed black line shown in Figure 10 is the remaining mortgage balance with the lower interest rate (5 per cent), under which the $100,000 loan is paid off in 21 years. The solid black line shows the remaining mortgage with the higher interest rate (6 per cent) under which the loan is repaid in 25 years with the same monthly repayments.

To establish the economic cost of the loan, we calculate the total cost of repaying the loan and compare it to the total value of the loan at the time it is repaid. Both the cost of the loan and its value go up automatically over time with inflation. The solid grey line shows the nominal value of the loan, with the dashed grey line the nominal cost of the repayments. The difference between the two at the time of final repayment

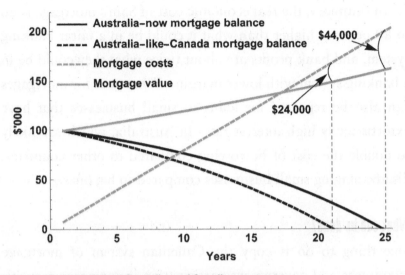

Figure 10: **Economic cost of Australian and Canadian mortgages**

gives an estimate of the economic cost of the loan. For the low interest rate mortgage, this cost is $24,000 and for the high one it is $44,000. This is the additional real economic cost that someone has had to pay for the privilege of borrowing money. The economic cost of the higher interest loan turns out to be 80 per cent higher than the lower interest loan.

Our example here is purely hypothetical, but the general point is that a seemingly small cost difference, of just 1 percentage point a year, turns out to be a huge cost difference over a period of decades, irrespective of other aspects of the loan situation. By the end of 2021 there were roughly $2 trillion of Australian mortgages out of a total of $3 trillion in bank lending. A bonus 1 percentage point margin on those loan balances is $30 billion per year, or $3000 for every Aussie household.

In summary, the real economic cost of Sam's mortgage is up to 80 per cent higher than what it could be in a fairer banking system, and bank profits are about twice what they could be in a banking system with lower margins. What goes for mortgages can also be repeated for loans to small businesses that have extortionately high interest rates in Australia, which are likely to double the cost of borrowing compared to other countries, disadvantaging small businesses compared to big ones.

What can be done?

One thing to do is copy the Canadian system of mortgage guarantees and government participation in mortgage securitisation, allowing those like Sam who do not own a share of the banks to regain a slice of Australia's banking profits. Or a step further still is to set up state competitors to private banks for the mortgage market. This is pro-competitive because private banks are ultimately producing a public good at the outset (i.e., money) and have implicit government guarantees behind them already, allowing them to coordinate as a monopoly through the mechanisms we describe that allow the Game of Mates to function.

Nicholas Gruen suggested such a scheme for Australia, copying proposals of others in the United Kingdom's Bank of England, whereby the central bank itself would compete in low-risk retail banking: for example, offering fee-free deposit accounts, and cheap mortgages for low-risk borrowers, such as those borrowing less than 60 per cent of their home value (Gruen, 2014). Such a change would be highly competitive in the sense that standardised commodity-style banking products would be offered at cost, providing retail bank opportunities to compete in more complex, and risky, lending and banking situations. After all, government bureaucracies can be quite good at offering standard products very cheaply; that is what governments do in education, health and policing too.

This solution follows our general recipe of taking the value of grey gifts off the table. By having the most low-risk loans and much of the deposit banking done by the state, the private banks will have fewer profits to use as gifts to executives, and fewer resources to influence politicians and the regulators. Their ability to blackmail the rest of society because of their money-creation monopoly is also removed.

A more difficult reform to accomplish is to encourage more private banks to compete with the Australian banks. It is notoriously difficult to cut into an existing home loan market, and, as we have discussed, newcomers are at a huge disadvantage. In addition to the struggle to grow, there is the risk of barriers being erected by incumbents, as we saw earlier from the reaction of the banks to Apple's entry to digital payment, or merger deals being done that undermine competition before it begins. The Jameses in Australian banking will fight hard against newcomers in their territory.

There are many things that should not be done. Though they sound good, they don't work. Additional transparency for instance, should not be expected to lead to any change. Nor should additional rules for switching fees or 'competitive neutrality' with other financial institutions be expected to have large effects. Having 'default packages' with respect to loans and mortgages is similarly pointless for they do not tackle the main driver of the high prices, which is the existing market power of the major banks, who will jointly determine defaults in any case.

Probably the worst thing to do is to give people public money to help them take on private loans, such as via 'first home buyer grants'. This merely increases the amount able to be borrowed by home buyers, increasing home prices, and costing the public billions in two ways: the public cost of the grants given, and the knock-on costs of the higher mortgages needed for new buyers across the market.

On a concluding note, a shift in public attitude is urgently needed. On the 25th anniversary of the privatisation of the CBA, the media celebrated the abnormally high gains made by investors who bought into the privatisation back in 1991 (Yates, 2016). But the reality is that the gains are a pure redistribution. Had the government owned the bank over the period, competing with other banks, those gains would have instead been made by the public at large through lower mortgage costs, or by the government, from their own profits on banking that could offset tax needs from elsewhere. Celebrating the CBA's uncommon profit is pure cheerleading for James, who owns the bank, and completely ignores that his success has come at the expense of bleeding Sam financially while Sam tries to buy a home.

10
A Cloak of Myths

There is one final ingredient in the Game of Mates. To properly hide the true nature of the Game to outsiders, James needs a plausible story that shows why it is good for society for him to control grey gifts, and how society benefits when he gives these gifts to his Mates. James hides behind these myths, using them like an umbrella to protect him from cleansing rains of serious public scrutiny. As the former head of Australian Chamber of Commerce and Industry, Peter Anderson said, 'the reform effort is frustrated by bad behaviour and the public [believing in] that bad behaviour' (Potter, 2016).

We have encountered several of James's myths so far: 'if we don't rezone land, no housing will be built'; 'governments must balance their budgets'; 'ageing is unaffordable unless people are forced to save'; and 'we need local expertise in our regulatory agencies'.

These myths never survive the most rudimentary logical reflection. One can simply reply that houses were built before zoning was invented and just because we now have rezoning decisions, doesn't mean they should be given for free. Or that government debts are private sector assets, and privatising income-producing government agencies deprives the government of future cash flows. Or that ageing is unaffordable if the forced savings accrue to James rather than the population doing the saving. And last, that we don't need local expertise because regulation is about technical knowledge and following rules, not teaming up with those we regulate.

Let us unpack the issue of myths in general though: who builds them; who propagates them; where you will find the adherents to them; what the myths do to the confidence of the public in the political system; and how myths eventually get challenged and overturned.

Think tanks are prime places where myths are created and deepened. The most widely known is probably the Institute of Public Affairs (IPA), funded from unknown sources and a breeding ground of Liberal Party politicians. Generalist think tanks like the IPA, which are not industry aligned, often hide their funding sources and comment on the activities of multiple industries and social policy, which makes them appear on the surface as a somewhat independent external party to many of James's Games.

There are now also institutes aligned with industries doing both lobbying and policy development, such as the Property Council of Australia, the Minerals Council of Australia, the Pharmacy Guild, and more. These have grown their political clout in the past few decades, so much so that they are another breeding ground for young Jameses who wish to play the Game as a career.

James also has strong allies promoting his myths in the media: in effect, another group of Mates. Even back in 2010, prior to the biggest changes in the news business and the most rapid declines in print journalism, a survey found that 55 per cent of articles were based on public relations handouts (Menadue and Keating, 2015). The news business is desperate to fill the space between its advertising, and James is happy to supply a flood of press releases and leaks, which make up a huge part of Sam's daily news diet.

Many journalists have tried to maintain their professional integrity and use their position to hold those in power to account, but as we have seen, such dissent is not tolerated by James and his Mates who are holding power.

Esteemed journalist Michael West spent his time at the *Sydney Morning Herald* as a senior business reporter, asking questions that rattled many Jameses and providing Sam with a glimpse of the many shady deals in transport, banking and other major sectors. He was shown the door in 2016 in a round of cost cutting that was a clear sign that James had taken hold, and that his myths could no longer be questioned in the media or his grey gifts scrutinised. It is no wonder Sam has a hard time seeing James's Game for what it truly is.

The rise of alternative online news sources on its face appears to be a huge benefit, but to us it mainly appears to be serving ever-smaller groups with their own loyalties and opinions. The United States is probably ahead of Australia in this regard, with its news landscape as polarised as its politics. James is fully aware of the splintering news landscape and we expect him to respond to this by spreading myths that are tailored to the political and social leaning of each audience in the new fractured media environment. Deep pockets buy you a lot of myths.

Of course, James and his Mates sometimes go too far and let the public see the true nature of political decisions and the cartel behaviour of James in business and politics. For example, when politicians try to funnel cars into tunnels owned by their Mates, it is a step too far, and the public sees the lie they have been fed. When a local developer gets a favour in their street, Sam sees the true nature of the Game up close. But for the average Sam, interrogating the nature of the Game stops there. Yet Sam has still seen it. Sam suspects the Game runs much deeper, but discovering its true extent is beyond Sam's grasp, as well as technical resources.

The myths of each group of Jameses are crafted to generate strong support from outside groups to make them appear more plausible, perhaps even from those groups who are losing out from James's favour-trading activities. To do this, they ensure that their Game is associated with a socially beneficial outcome, even if an objective view shows that their economic interests are completely opposed. This means they capture words deemed noble by society. Whatever is thought of as safe and good starts to be the clothing of James and his Mates who wrap themselves in a myth that from the outside looks to all appearances exactly like what is good for society. James's rhetoric is full of words such as ethics, free competition, social values, responsibility, benefits to the average Australian and so forth. Yet James means the exact opposite with his use of these words to what the average Australian does. He twists these words to make his favour-trading activities seem acceptable. To be frank, James uses pretty much the same words we use in this book, but he means quite different things by them when he puts them into practice.

We can see how these myths can cement the power of James and his Mates. It is now totally normal for property developers to be seen as the major stakeholders of interest when discussing affordable housing policy. And yet their economic interest is the exact opposite. They would be fools to flood the market at low prices, as they say they will if they get favourable zoning deci-sions. Yet, by cloaking themselves in the language of distorted economics and social values, they are now in the driver's seat.

Myth promotion is also a good way for potential new Jameses to signal their wish to join the Game. So ambitious newcomers will be amongst the most fanatical proponents of myths: the lickspittles speak with their master's tongue.

The need for myths, and the need to be associated with everything that sounds good and proper, also tells you where you are most likely to find James and his Mates inside your organisation. Expect to see James in the communication depart-ments, right-to-information offices, integrity offices, complaints departments, internal investigation units and social outreach. For unless James can find 'useful idiots' to staff such departments (people gullible enough to not see his Game), he needs people he can trust to do his bidding in these positions; people who will propagate his myths and protect him from actual scrutiny.

This is particularly true for anything that looks like transparency and internal investigations, which are both an acute danger to James. Independent thinkers in such departments are a danger that he needs to eliminate and that you should hence not expect to survive in those places.

One side effect of James's myth-making activities is that many of the next generation of publicly minded folk end up genuinely believing James's lies. This means they can be seduced into playing the Game in their sector of the economy without ever questioning whether the way things are being done creates public benefits. It means that when these folk end up working for the regulators, they already believe that making rules in the interest of James and his Mates is in the interest of the public, allowing them to participate in the Game without realising. They are rewarded for their activities, which only serves to reinforce their erroneous beliefs.

A result is that James gets away with his Game very easily in many areas, and the average citizen only slowly develops a general cynicism of the whole elite, being unable to identify who is good and who is bad. A general feeling of betrayal emerges. These feelings can be tapped by outsider politicians like Donald Trump, Pauline Hanson, Clive Palmer and by those who campaigned for Brexit in the United Kingdom. Random anger emerges at anything that looks like money and the establishment. Wild conspiracy theories emerge from people who know just enough to know that they are being fleeced, but who cannot quite see the individual elements of how this happens and thus latch on to a story of grand conspiracies, missing the reality that

James's Game is an emergent characteristic of the natural human tendency to form groups through reciprocal trades in favours.

The fact that James and his Mates automatically corrupt the language in a society, turning the actual content of the best words into the worst practice, adds to the general confusion and cynicism, ultimately leading to culture wars. This also helps to explain why reforms come in cycles. A population must be so fed up with the current situation that they are willing to invest in a new language that comes from outside and seek new sources of information and advice outside their usual fare.

We thus think that the creation of myths, their propagation and their general 'fogging' effect on the Australian population ensure that reforms come only in cycles when the course of reality reveals the true nature of the myths being told. By outlining the core elements of James's Game, we hope to stimulate others to seek out new information and find a new language and new platforms to lift the fog and foster the next wave of reforms.

11
Other Games, Other Mates

James plays many, many Games in addition to the ones we have looked at so far. Some of the smaller Games still richly reward James at the expense of Sam, as we can see by taking a quick glance at the Games of Taxes; Pharmacies, Medicines and Health; Agriculture; Taxis; Supermarkets; and University Education.

Taxes

We have not yet touched on the billions of dollars in annual taxes dodged by multinationals that are infiltrating the Game of Mates in Australia. Since these companies are largely foreign-owned, this directly costs Australians, increasing the taxes the rest of us must pay. Partly this low taxation is due to low levels of company tax rates, but largely it is because of favourable tax regulations. Australia has the largest 'tax expenditures'— which are legal loopholes that provide tax discounts to select groups—in the OECD. Italy tried hard, but only came in second place (Tyson, 2014). But it's worse. In 2019–20, 33 per cent of the biggest 2400 companies in Australia paid no taxes at all (Australian Taxation Office, 2022). So extensive is tax minimisation (evasion) by large corporates that journalist Michael West hilariously publishes a 'Tax Dodgers Awards', publicising companies that pay zero tax. In 2021, companies like ExxonMobil, Vodafone, Virgin Australia, Peabody (the coal-miner) and Amcor had paid no tax for six years in a row. The same was true for 29 out of Michael West's 40 awarded tax dodgers, despite $519 billion of incomes over that period and generating huge returns for shareholders (West, 2021). Veteran corporate tax accountant and whistle-blower George Rozvany estimates that international corporations manage to dodge about $50 billion in taxes a year in Australia by using various accounting tricks (Long, 2016).

The details of the tax system increasingly favour the richest, though the mechanisms can be difficult to see for ordinary Australians. Take the issue of franking credits, which were introduced in 1987. To see how they work, consider that Australia's profitable banks paid $12 billion of tax on their profits in 2021, a form of corporate taxation. The banks pay out a similar amount in dividends to their shareholders. Those dividends are then accompanied by franking credits, which represent the amount of taxes paid by the company. Individuals can use those franking credits to offset the taxes they would have to pay on other incomes. Since company share ownership is highly skewed to the wealthy, these credits favour shareholding by the rich (Richardson, 2018).

Tax dodges for James and his Mates also come in the form of accounting tricks like family trusts, where non-wage incomes can be divided up between family members to reduce tax liability. This lurk is worth it for those with very high incomes, like James and his Mates, who thus reduce their tax liability by billions. In 2017, federal Opposition leader Bill Shorten announced a policy to tax all money distributed through trust structures like company profits, with a 30 per cent tax rate, which was expected to raise nearly $2 billion per year (Thomsen, 2017).

There are also discounts on capital gains taxes of 50 per cent, primarily benefiting James and his Mates at the top end of town, and costing roughly $9 billion per year in lost tax revenue, according to the Treasury budget assessment.

There have been minor improvements. The federal government instituted a 'diverted profits tax' in the 2016–17 budget and funded a 'Tax Avoidance Taskforce' in order to slow the flow of untaxed profits from Australia by multinationals with over $1 billion in turnover. In 2019 the ATO assessed 142 companies to be liable for $1.9 billion under these rules. The tax office had raised $9 billion in taxes from these provisions since the advent of the new tax up until the end of 2019 (Khadem, 2019). A small win for Sam.

In 2021, around 140 countries agreed to a global 15 per cent minimum tax on corporate profits. This sounds good, but we have reservations about its practical effect in the long run. Such agreements are notoriously hard to enforce and depend on definitions of profits and offsets that are easy to game. The 15 per cent minimum agreement also forestalls much more aggressive forms of taxation, like the French 'digitax' which consisted essentially of sending Big Tech companies a tax bill based on estimated turnover in France. Former US president Donald Trump successfully threatened France with a trade war in 2019 to get that tax off the table, showing how deeply international politics is interwoven with taxation. Also, 15 per cent corporate tax for many countries means a substantial tax reduction on companies, which means someone else will have to pay more tax. It is thus not clear at the time of writing whether the international corporate profit agreement is a win for Sam or for James.

A longer term trend in taxation that has favoured James (and for which he has lobbied hard) is the overall shift of taxation away from wealth and financial assets. For example, in 1968, inheritance taxes in Australia were around 0.6 per cent of GDP, or 3.1 per cent of total tax revenue. This tax, which applies predominantly to the wealthiest individuals, is a direct way to distribute any gains to James, ill-gotten or not, back to Sam. In economic terms, this tax is both equitable and efficient. But by 1989 the tax was completely disbanded, as it was also in the United States, but not across Europe.

If inheritance taxes remained today as they were in the 1960s, they would be expected to generate at least the same share of GDP, given the rising wealth inequality since that period. Using 2014–15 data, 0.6 per cent of GDP is $10 billion, or 2.8 per cent of federal tax revenue. Instead of paying tax, this economic value instead goes to various groups of Jameses who own most of the country's assets and wealth. In fact, in 2014–15

Belgium and France raised a similar proportion of inheritance tax revenues to what Australia did in the 1960s, so it is not a fantasy to suggest that such taxes could once again be effectively implemented, given the political will.

Adding together the tax dodges of multinationals (up to $50 billion), tax lurks from trusts (around $1 billion), discounts on capital gains (about $9 billion) and the loss of inheritance taxes (about $10 billion) that are primarily advantageous to James and his Mates, we get a ballpark estimate of $70 billion in reduced federal taxes that are instead covered by taxes on Sam's income. To cover this shortfall, Sam pays around 23 per cent extra in federal taxes.

Pharmacies, medicines and health

Pharmacy retailers and drug companies have their own Game of Mates as well. In his assessment of the most powerful lobbyists in the country, journalist Matthew Knott commented, 'if you're looking for power that's concentrated, power that's embedded in our political system and power that's wielded through intimidation, not just persuasion, then Kos is your man' (Knott, 2011).

For nearly three decades, Australia's most powerful lobbyist, Kos Sclavos, has represented the Pharmacy Guild of Australia, a lobby group working on behalf of the 4000 owners of pharmacy stores in the country. Kos is James writ large. And he and his Mates are so entrenched in the health policy of the country that it makes it very difficult to even notice their activities.

The Pharmacy Guild has been one of the country's most reliable political donors for over two decades and has managed to ensure its monopoly position is protected, despite repeated reviews and government inquiries that have suggested the pharmacy monopoly be broken. That multimillion-dollar windfall to the 4000 pharmacy owners Kos represents is a grey gift that comes at a cost to the most vulnerable in society, who pay through higher health expenses.

The government protections for pharmacy retailers come from two main regulations. First, in the form of licensing controls over who can own a pharmacy, requiring only a licensed pharmacist to be able to own a pharmacy, which protects these pharmacy owners from corporate competition. The second protection is in the form of elaborate and arbitrary location restrictions on the establishment of new pharmacies, which limit local competition.[32] Figure 11 shows just how strange these location restrictions are in practice, with limits on proximity to supermarkets of a particular size, and to a specified number of doctors.

Like other Mates, pharmacists hide their game by cloaking it in the language of public safety. For example, the subtitle of the Pharmacy Board of Australia's member summary of relevant regulations is 'Regulating Pharmacists—Managing Risk to the Public'. Yet none of the regulations that grant massive economic gains to a selected group of pharmacy-owning Jameses in this sector is remotely relevant to reducing risk to the public. Quite the opposite in fact. With fewer pharmacies spaced further apart and more expensive than they need to be, the risk that

Part 2—Applications not involving cancellation of existing approval

Item	Column 1 Application kind	Column 2 Requirements
	Applications not involving cancellation of existing approval	
130	New pharmacy (at least 1.5 km)	(a) the proposed premises are at least 1.5 km, in a straight line, from the nearest approved premises; and (b) the Authority is satisfied that, at all relevant times, there is, within 500 m, in a straight line, from the proposed premises, either: 　(i) both the equivalent of at least one full–time prescribing medical practitioner and a supermarket that has a gross leasable area of at least 1,000 m²; or 　(ii) a supermarket that has a gross leasable area of at least 2,500 m²
131	New pharmacy (at least 10 km)	The proposed premises are at least 10 km, by the shortest lawful access route, from the nearest approved premises
132	New additional pharmacy (at least 10 km)	(a) the proposed premises are: 　(i) in the same town as an approved premises; and 　(ii) at least 200 m, in a straight line, from the nearest approved premises; and 　(iii) at least 10 km, by the shortest lawful access route, from any approved premises other than the approved premises mentioned in subparagraph (ii); and (b) the Authority is satisfied that, at all relevant times, in the same town as the proposed premises are: 　(i) the equivalent of at least 4 full–time prescribing medical practitioners practising; and 　(ii) one or 2 supermarkets that have a combined total gross leasable area of at least 2,500 m²
133	New pharmacy in a designated complex (small shopping centre)	The proposed premises: (a) are in a small shopping centre; and (b) are at least 500 m, in a straight line, from the nearest approved premises, other than approved premises in a large shopping centre or private hospital; and

Figure 11: **Legal protections against competition for pharmacists**

Sam cannot easily get medicines, or even afford them, is hugely increased. It is hence another case of James capturing the meaning of words to hide his true economic interests.

Two cases show clearly that the guild hides its economic interest behind straight-faced lies about protecting the public from risks of 'cowboy' outfits dispensing prescription drugs. Back in 2011, the guild, on behalf of its member pharmacy owners, received payments from the vitamin supplement company Blackmores, in an arrangement that ensured that pharmacy computer systems would prompt them to 'discuss a Blackmores Companion range product with patients picking up a prescription for one of four popular medications'. Essentially, they implemented systematic upselling of supplements that have no sound medical justification from a favoured supplier (Harvey, 2011a). To any Sam seeing this happen, the guild appears to be acting like the cowboy it argues it is protecting the public from.

And would you believe it, but immediately after this controversy, the guild signed up to take commissions of $7 per patient from multinational drug company Pfizer for enrolling their customers in Pfizer's 'support programs', which involved periodic email reminders that encourage healthy activities, including taking medication sold by Pfizer (Harvey, 2011b). Customers who sign up are not advised about the commission received by the pharmacy. Yet, when a 2015 government review noted that the economic protections for pharmacists should be removed, the guild then hid behind the claim that it would 'compromise patient care' (Donelly, 2015; Harper et al., 2015).

In 2017 the guild was able to secure $210 million compensation from the government because of lower than forecast prescription volumes, an astonishing move (Australian Government, 2018).

Just how much does this all cost? Since 1992, pharmacy mark-ups have increased from 25 per cent to 34 per cent of their costs for dispensing prescription drugs. The Pharmacy Guild negotiates directly with government the fees the public will pay them to dispense prescription drugs, which seem as arbitrary as the other location and ownership protections granted to pharmacy owners. The last audit of these fees came to $2.4 billion in 2013–14 (Auditor General, 2015). Even a 10 per cent cost reduction here would return $240 million per year to Sam, away from James. Together with shrinking mark-ups back to 1992 levels, there is easily scope for $420 million per year to be taken away from these select 4000 pharmacy-owning Jameses.

One may look incredulously at how blatantly the pharmacies rort the system, but even their efforts are small potatoes compared to how much the pharmaceutical companies manage to get via unnecessarily high prices for their medicines. A 2017 comparison of medicine found even after substantial attempts in 2016 to reduce pharmaceutical prices that 'Australia's drug prices remain more than twice that of the UK, and 3.6 times higher than New Zealand's' (Duckett, 2017). Prior to that, the rip-offs were much worse.

In 2011, Australia spent more than double what New Zealand spent on pharmaceuticals per capita. Australia spent US$587 (around 22% more than the Organisation for Economic Co-operation and Development (OECD) average) while New Zealand spent US$288 (around 40% less than the OECD average). A 2011–12 analysis of the 73 individual drug-dose combinations that are prescribed the most often or account for the most expenditure in Australia showed that Australian prices were, on average, eight times higher than New Zealand's. (Babar and Vitry, 2014)

It seems that Kiwis have for decades spent about half as much on medicine as we do, paying an astonishing one-eighth to one-fifth of the price for the most-prescribed drugs, and with no noticeably worse health outcomes.

The reason this can occur is because decisions about pricing and subsidisation of medicines are negotiated through opaque channels, and with some discretion, which is an environment ripe for a Game of Mates. Many of the policies designed to increase the government's negotiating power with pharmaceutical companies have been watered down over time, with each change offering a grey gift to the drug companies. While there have been some minor recent changes tipping the balance in favour of the government, estimates are that we overpay upwards of $500 million per year, potentially as high as $1.3 billion because of poorly designed and implemented drug pricing policies (Duckett, 2017; Duckett, 2013a).

And what is the obvious remedy to save the Australian taxpayer roughly $1 billion a year? To essentially adopt the New Zealand system, which has an independent statutory body called the Pharmaceutical Management Agency (Pharmac), whose sole objective is to use their defined budget effectively to ensure good health outcomes from access to pharmaceuticals. They focus on negotiating lower prices with drug companies, and promoting optimal use of drugs to keep costs down to only that necessary for effective medical treatment. It should not be hard for Australia to adopt a similar system.

One should of course not be surprised to learn that the pharmaceutical lobby includes many a former politician and top health department civil servant, swapping hats between the supposed regulator and the regulated. John Menadue, who analysed the workings of 266 lobbyist organisations in Canberra, summarised the inner workings of health policy in Australia as follows. 'The health "debate" in Australia is really between the minister and the Australian Medical Association, the Australian Pharmacy Guild, Medicines Australia and the Private Health Insurance companies. The debate is not with the public about health policy and strategy; it is about how the minister and the department manage the vested interests' (Menadue and Keating, 2015).

Private health insurance is another area where repeated political decisions have been grey gifts for wealthy private insurers. Tax advantages given to people who take out private health insurance, for example, have been a subsidy of $7 billion a year for the past decade (about $1–2 billion in tax expenditure and $6 billion in rebates) (Duckett and Nemet, 2019). The private health insurance market duplicates many public hospital services, while scraping nearly $2.4 billion in profits each year as its customers are funnelled into its schemes by regulatory incentives its members designed (APRA, 2021). It has been long known that the cost of performing many of these hospital services in the public system instead is just 40 per cent of the cost in the private system (Cheng, 2013). For every dollar in reduced subsidy (rebate) to private health insurance, the additional cost to the public hospital system is just $0.40, providing a $0.60 overall saving. On the total $6 billion in rebates, that's a $3.6 billion saving each year.

Altogether, there are groups of Jameses in all parts of our health system, costing Sam billions: around $420 million to pharmacists, up to $1.3 billion to drug companies and around $3.6 billion to private health insurers.

What might break down James's Game in pharmacies is competition from other major industries. Supermarkets are themselves powerful groups who have an interest in capturing these gains for themselves. Two retail conglomerates, Wesfarmers and Woolworths, were reported at the end of 2021 to be looking to purchase the Australian Pharmaceutical Industries, a large pharmacy wholesaler and corporate owner of various chain-store pharmacies. Though these companies will have their own interests in limiting competition in the long run, there is a chance that they will use their political clout to remove some of the more egregious regulatory barriers to competition in this sector in the meantime. Time will tell.

Agriculture

One of the most historically successful groups of Jameses is Australia's farmers. They have also created some of the most successful myths to hide their Game from Sam. For example, despite being one of the wealthiest groups in the country, with 70 per cent of farming households falling in the top 20 per cent of the country's wealthiest, the slogan 'every family needs a farmer' is widely recognised and repeated. That slogan was crafted by the farmers' lobby group AgForce to promote sympathy from city dwellers and reinforce the notion that country living is a challenge. But the reverse slogan—every farmer needs a family—would be more socially justifiable given the economic reality.

The Jameses in agriculture are also partly to blame for the public's limited understanding of topics such as 'domestic food security', a phrase often used as a scare tactic when agricultural incomes are threatened. James cloaks himself with this myth when it suits, but at other times is happy to boast about how he and his Mates export 60 per cent of our food production, indicating that it would be almost impossible for domestic food supplies to be threatened. Because of the prevalence of these myths, Sam has mixed feelings about food prices. When the price of milk falls, for example, the media, and Sam, start worrying about the livelihood of farmers, as if farming livelihoods are sacred totems that the country should worship, respect and defend. These myths have turned farming from a business into a sacred emblem of the country.

Behind the veil of these successful myths, many valuable grey gifts have been traded amongst James and his Mates in politics. Examples of grey gifts include: Queensland's ethanol scheme, which has been contrived to prop up local demand for sugar and wheat; the Murray–Darling Basin buyback scheme, which bought water rights from farmers that never existed (there were more water rights than water); farm tax breaks enacted in 2015; along with systematic drought relief that has cost the federal government alone $8 billion in the first two decades of the 21st century (Wright and Bagshaw, 2019).

Programs that provide cash handouts and debt relief during drought are a type of free insurance provided to farmers from

Sam, but not provided to others. As the economist John Freebairn puts it: 'It socialises losses, so whenever (farmers) have a drought, they get some handouts from the Government; whenever they're in good seasons they keep the profits' (Vidot and Barbour, 2014; quoting John Freebairn). This type of one-way street of rights without obligations is a common feature of hidden grey gifts that are at the heart of the Game of Mates, as they are very easy to politically enact.

The one-sided nature of regulations in agriculture also applies to international trade. While seeking to open up foreign markets, some farmers have also lost protections from imports, but not all. In the case of bananas, the farmers are still able to export, but are protected from competing with imports, an argument they support with stories of needing to keep out banana plant diseases, another widely used myth. The fact that bananas are not native to Australia and that the supposedly feared foreign diseases to banana plants are already in Australia are conveniently hidden from sight whenever the public is fed the myth (Foster, Frijters and Ko, 2018).

What is interesting about the last decade in agriculture is the way the group dynamics of the Game of Mates in that sector evolved. First, due to competition between agricultural sectors themselves, and second, due to competition with other groups of Jameses in other sectors, such as mining and gas.

In legislation enacted in 2015, Queensland required all fuels sold in the state to contain 3 per cent ethanol, with the ethanol coming from grains and sugar. This was a grey gift, increasing prices and demand by creating a captive local market for ethanol from local grain. However, other parts of agriculture would now have to compete with ethanol producers for local grain. Feedlot cattle farmers in areas producing ethanol lost out and campaigned against the law to support their own 'agricultural sub-interests'. They competed against other farmers. While in this case the legislation passed, the splintering of a unified group of Jameses with a common interest diminishes their power by putting them in competition with each other.

Taxis

We have certainly not exhausted all the sectors where James and his Mates have successfully played their Game in Australia. The taxi industry, for example, was a protected monopoly for decades. State regulations ensured that new quotas of taxi licences were created only if they did not depress the market price of existing taxi licences. Because of this, the value of taxi licences was around $6 billion in 2014, yet it was purely a private monopoly created for the benefit of a handful of major taxi licence–owning Jameses (Deloitte, 2013; Murray, 2014). About 16 per cent of the cost of every taxi ride goes to James.

Despite years of technical advice from inside the public service about removing James's privileges, the Game of Mates in the taxi industry was only broken by the entry of deep-pocketed foreign competitors willing to break the law in order to change it. This was Uber and other 'ride-hailing' services.

Even here we have a problem—a potential new group of Jameses whose interests are to defraud the public. Uber's business model relied to some degree on tax avoidance by drivers to make its system work. By 2015 the Australia Tax Office had cracked down on this and required Uber drivers to register themselves as a business and charge GST, equalising the playing field. The ACT enacted laws incorporating Uber and others into its standard regulations, forcing drivers to register and license their car with a yearly fee, which went some way to ensuring that one group of Jameses was not replaced by another, and the public interest was preserved.

Uber took years to offer any assistance to the tax authorities about disclosing its own profits on their Australian business. However, by 2017 the tax avoidance issues appeared to have been resolved and the main effect of Uber and other similar companies was to break down the regulatory barrier for competition in taxi services. Though not as cheap as when they first entered the market, the entry of ride-sharing businesses appears to have undercut much of the 16 per cent of each fare that previously went to the taxi licence–owning Jameses.

Like we saw in agriculture, the lesson here is that a Game of Mates is rarely unwound in an industry from inside with cordial negotiations. It usually takes an external threat.

To be clear: the threat from Uber was not a technological one. Though many people think technology is the great disruptor, Uber would never have disrupted the taxi industry if it had the technology only, but was not willing to break the law to improve its bargaining position. Indeed, Australia's main taxi companies already had mobile booking apps years before Uber arrived in the country. Uber helped its drivers dodge taxes and had the advantage that most taxi customers, and theirs, were from wealthy parts of society, ensuring that the reduced cost of Uber and its fight against authorities (which ended up increasing both its reputation and the taxes paid by its drivers) was front-page news.

Supermarkets

A similar experience of a new foreign competitor taking away the power of James occurred in the supermarket sector. The dominant Woolworths and Coles duopoly had for decades exerted tremendous power over shopping mall landlords, local suppliers, town planning and many other hidden regulations. At one time these two retailers had a 90 per cent market share. Like in the taxi industry, it took a deep-pocketed outsider, this time in the form of Aldi, to finally begin to undermine the power base of the 'Colesworths' duopoly.

Like all Jameses before them, they went down fighting. For example, the duopolists tried to force Aldi to sign up to regulations and industry standards that were designed to protect their own interests. This included the Grocery Code of Conduct, which was totally unsuitable to Aldi's store format and supply chain (King, 2013). They also challenged Aldi over own-label packaging that resembled name brands in colour and style (Mitchell, 2013). And they used their power over long-term leases in shopping malls to commit mall owners to restrict potential competitor supermarkets from being established in the same mall, a practice that was stamped out as anti-competitive by the ACCC. After these fights, Aldi thus managed to enter into the market, growing to over 500 stores in 2022, and opened the door for more foreign supermarkets like US bulk grocery retailer Costco, which had one store in Australia in 2009 and thirteen stores by 2021.

Research by the RBA suggests that new competition in grocery retailing has reduced the inflation of food prices by 2 per cent per year since 2010, or 13 per cent overall in their six-year study period, which gives an indication of how much the Jameses in the supermarket sector were previously stealing from Sam every time Sam fed the family (Ballantyne and Langcake, 2016). As in the taxi industry, the entry of new competitors with their own interests was required to break down the power of James in that sector.

University education

James's takeover of the university sector in the 2000s was the result of swarming around a valuable grey gift: the power to choose how to use the valuable government land that was given to universities. He could, for example, make deals with property developers who wanted to build on university land via leasing arrangements, a form of selling off the land without officially being the case. He could also build dormitories for students on campus, still one of the most lucrative things universities do. He could build parking lots and rent out spaces. He could have commercial companies rent premises on campuses. And of course, he could also teach students for much less money than before by having very large classes and second-rate teachers. James's only real problem was to break the power of the academics running the show.

In hindsight, taking control of the university system turned out to be relatively easy. Once James took over in one university and showed the people running the other universities what sort of lucrative outcomes could be achieved when you were in charge, the academics in charge of the other places joined James with remarkable speed, or they simply invited James to repeat the trick at their campus.

It was the initial takeover that was the hardest. James had to get himself and his Mates close to the top of the university. The only real way to do that was to take advantage of the fact that governments were already loaded with groups of Jameses and held the power to appoint the top people at universities. By ingratiating himself with politicians, building up from exchanges of small favours to ever larger ones (for example, 'I educate your kids and write reports for you that no one else will; you help me out') he managed to gain positions at the top of the university hierarchy. You might very well think that university was in Queensland, but we could not possibly comment.

Once near the top, James's job of pushing out the real academics and making sure they would never be able to come back was easy. After all, real academics are usually clueless about the Game of Mates; some people say that is why they became academics in the first place. All James had to do was leak a few lies about the academics in charge, bully them around and make their life difficult by overloading them with dull non-academic work. They soon left university management of their own accord, leaving James and his Mates in charge.

Ensuring the academics never came back was also simple. University senates, which in a legal sense own the university, were once stacked full of academics, but vice-chancellors and their machinery had strong inputs on who could get into the senates and were able to slowly change the rules governing member-ship. James made sure to remove academics, with only one in six university senate members now holding a PhD. He managed to whittle 'academic staff representation' down to usually no more than one or two on a senate of 20 to 30 people. And he put his own Mates in senior management onto the senates as well. More interestingly, he stacked it full of representatives of groups with no understanding of universities at all—students, business community interest group members, secretaries, cleaners, human resources and more. They all got their representative, and turned out to be the easiest targets for James to mislead. By presenting himself as the guy in charge, sending them stacks of information they did not have the time or the expertise to read, he could count on their natural obedience to go along with whatever he suggested. He executed this beautiful strategy perfectly. James thus successfully stacked the senates, the bodies that legally own the universities and that supposedly employ him and decide on his salary, with Mates, lickspittles and simpletons.

After that, it was plain sailing. James increased his own salary to levels unseen anywhere else in Western academia, hitting over $1 million per year on average by 2019.[33] He hired legions of administrators to keep the academics off his back by keeping them busy with compliance, regardless of its relevance to research or teaching, the main objective being to keep the academics docile. He reduced teaching standards, and he found plenty of ways to make additional money for him and his Mates from the university. Now James and his Mates totally dominate every university in Australia, and the basic tricks described above are pretty apt for the way many large schools and institutions like hospitals succumb to James's Game too.

As a result of this Game, construction has soared on campuses. After all, as we have seen before, there is no corruption quite as lucrative as corruption in property development, and universities are sitting on prime property. Relieved of any restraint on teaching and quality of student outcomes, students were let in in droves to buy their degrees, preferably without having to be taught much.

University James had the amazing luck of discovering a new source of money in the 1990s and 2000s, something no one expected beforehand, but that cemented his position greatly. He discovered the visa-selling game, where he could charge foreign students a premium price, and sell them a degree regardless of whether they had learnt anything, which would virtually ensure them an Australian visa. Plenty of wealthy foreign families wanted their children to be citizens in Australia, and were quite willing to pay the necessary fees to use this method for access.

James discovered a goldmine with these students, charging huge fees for second-rate courses, fleecing them further with his on-campus accommodation, and with additional entry years during which they were taught English. The government loved him for it, encouraging him to take on more and more foreign students, quite happily allowing him to kill off any remaining power the academics had since those pesky academics were much less keen on the visa-selling game. James made himself indispensable to governments wanting the influx of rich foreigners whilst himself getting rich from it too. Just how important these students are to the Game in the university sector was on display in 2020 when pandemic border closers put a stop to these activities. They lobbied to quickly reopen borders and have special charter flights and quarantine rules for students.

The cost to society of this Game comes from universities squandering resources by being exceptionally inefficient in their core functions of teaching and research and by having droves of unnecessary administrators whose main function is to keep James in power.

To get an idea of these costs we can compare what an efficient university looks like with the average Australian one. Looking at nearly 150 universities in the 2008–09 period in the United States, Martin and Hill (2012) concluded that the most efficient institutions that had core research and teaching functions had around three academics per two administrators.

To be clear: the number of administrators in US universities has also increased a lot over the decades, doubling in the last 30 years. Partly this is because these universities are chasing alumni money and hiring staff for sports, which are not major activities in Australian universities. Partly, of course, the United States has its own Jameses to worry about.

How do Australian universities compare in terms of efficiency? We set research assistants to the task of checking the phonebooks of universities to see how many people working there were doing academic jobs (teaching, research), and found that each academic has one-and-a-half to two administrative counterparts on average. That means that for every academic, compared to the benchmark of US research and teaching universities, there are twice as many more administrators than necessary. On top of that increased waste in terms of unnecessary administrators, it is also the case that the time academic staff spend on administrative tasks has also grown to be around 25 per cent of their time, mostly to 'comply' with regulations set by the administration staff.

Add the surplus administrators to the additional time the academics now spend on unproductive activities, as well as the additional costs made on bureaucracies at the ministries and the grant agencies, and you are getting close to half of the costs being wasted in the university sector. In other words, our tertiary education is twice as expensive as it should be. And indeed, in Northern European countries like Germany, local students pay far less for universities (around $5000 per student per year) than they do here, particularly the students in master's-level courses who easily pay $40,000 a year for desirable courses like medicine.[34]

The enormous bureaucratic layer has now also infiltrated the institutions around universities. Grant-giving agencies, such as the Australian Research Council and the National Health and Medical Research Council also caught on to the trick that they could spend the money they were supposed to give to academics on themselves by simply making it more complicated for academics to apply for grants. With more requirements came more paperwork and many more administrators. Grant applications for relatively small amounts (such as \$100,000) went from small forms of a few pages to whole booklets of hundreds of pages, just like what happened in the United States.

A return to a more academic mindset would be very difficult to achieve with so much money pouring into our universities and being captured to use as grey gifts traded amongst senior staff and their counterparts in government. The basic solution must revolve around taking away the value of these grey gifts. One way is to separate the visa-selling activities from teaching domestic students, and to charge the visa-selling outfits the full value of their activities. If Australia wants to sell its visas via education, that is fine in principle, but let the average Australians then benefit from that by taxing the profits that are made, since what is sold (visas) is owned by all Australians.

Similarly, universities can be charged rents by the state or federal governments for all non-core activities on campus, such as residential accommodation and parking.

More radical would be to truly privatise the management of universities, such as by offering leases to foreign universities for running local ones. Much like access to cable television can be leased by cities to prospective cable television providers, so too could governments make money off universities by allowing foreign universities to bid up for the right to run a local one for some time. This would copy the example of some sectors in Australia, where outsiders with deep pockets have gradually managed to muscle James out of his elevated position, such as the example earlier when Aldi gradually started to compete with Woolworths and Coles. Obviously the contracts would be complicated, but it is not all that different from having foreign banks and insurance companies operate in Australia.

The worst thing that can be done is a halfway form of privatisation, where James is left unchallenged in his position but is given more leeway to charge more to local students, who often have nowhere else they can realistically go to because they need to keep living with their parents due to high housing costs. 'Fee deregulation' can be more aptly described as a licence for James to extract more cash from local students.[35]

We can also learn from the efforts of other countries. The Netherlands limits the salaries of the top managers to that of their prime minister. In Australia, the average salary of the top 39 university vice-chancellors dropped back below its $1 million peak the prior year to $985,000 in 2020 (Smith, 2020), far higher than the prime minister's salary of $550,000, and to us, evidence that grey gifts are being traded at the top of university administrations. Pegging top salaries at universities should deter James from entering the senior positions, leaving them open to people who care more about education and research. Yet, the opportunities for favouritism are so immense, and so routinely taken now in Australia, that this measure is unlikely to quickly undo the current situation.

Another means of breaking the current stranglehold that James has over the university sector is to have the top jobs like vice-chancellors appointed by citizen juries rather than via ministers for education and the cliques of insiders that hang around university management. The prime thing the cliques and ministers look for in a new person for a top position in a university is that they don't upset the gravy train, something that random citizens will neither be aware of nor care about. Obviously, current university management would fight such a change to the appointment system.

We think it will be very hard to have effective university reform whilst there are enormous surplus funds on the table from foreign students and property ownership. Options to capture the surplus include having the government charge foreign students directly for studying in Australia, and having universities then competitively bid to give them spaces, which effectively means the community as a whole pockets the value of the visas that attract students to Australia.

An option to take the property game out of universities is for university land to directly fall under a for-profit public firm, with universities having to rent land from those entities. One can object to this by noting that this would turn profitable universities into loss-making enterprises because all the profits would go to the public firms owning the land. Yet the separating of land and educational activities would merely make visible what the profitable parts and the education parts are, which in turn would simply force governments into subsidising the remaining education arms of universities to the degree necessary to get the number of university students the community wants.

The political response to the 2020 pandemic provides clues as to how change may come about. The JobKeeper wage subsidy program available to private employers who saw downturns in revenue created qualifying rules that appeared designed to explicitly exclude universities. What this shows is that on the right of Australian politics there is some animus towards the university sector, perhaps due to its growing cultural and political influence on the political left. Hence we can expect that if any serious changes are proposed they will come from the political right and will be vehemently opposed by the left of politics, alongside the university administration who benefit from the way things are.

Other sectors

Other groups of Jameses are infiltrating the hospital and school education sectors, where Australia has historically performed admirably by international standards. Public private partnerships (PPP) for schools are now being rolled out, enabling James and his Mates to avoid bidding on competitively priced construction contracts, but to build, own and maintain school buildings and facilities for 30 years with the state government paying him a guaranteed rate of return on costs. In Queensland there have been seventeen PPP schools so far completed under two PPP contracts (Department of Education, 2022). It is a way to funnel public money into James and his Mates' hands without them putting any of their own money at risk, and the games played in the PPP infrastructure sector are likely to be repeated here.

PPP hospitals are another way in which James has tried to funnel money into the hands of his Mates in the past few decades in Australia. The same tricks of opaque contracts and implicit government guarantees are all there, and many of these PPP hospitals have been bought back by state governments because of repeated contractual failures (Duckett, 2013b). The PPP Northern Beaches Hospital in Sydney, for example, was meant to save the state money and hassle, but it cost twice as much as initially promised, and, when opened in 2018, had critical equipment and staff shortages that led to the resignation of the CEO and a parliamentary inquiry into the PPP contract details. (Davies, 2018; NSW Parliament, 2020).

The Game of Mates also has a global dimension. For example, Australia's former Foreign Investment Review Board (FIRB) chairman Brian Wilson, a former investment banker, accepted a senior advisory role with US private equity financial company Carlyle Group in September 2016. He did so without resigning from his government post, where his role is to monitor investment activities in Australia by foreign entities. During this time the FIRB approved the $9.7 billion sale of the Port of Melbourne to a consortium of local and foreign investment funds (Danckert, 2016). After intense media scrutiny of this arrangement, Wilson did suspend his appointment at Carlyle Group until after he left the FIRB, though these actions show just how blatant the Game of Mates has become, and how little oversight or enforcement there is (Ryan, 2016).

In telecommunications, Australians have forked out tens of billions of dollars to prop up the now-private monopolist provider of copper wiring, Telstra. Adam Schwab detailed in his 2010 book, *Pigs at the Trough,* how the ministries and the company managed to shift the policy environment in its favour, allowing the new crop of Telstra executives to increase their own salaries without facing any real competition. The public efforts to invest in a new fibre-optic infrastructure through the National Broadband Network (NBN) were frustrated by the Game of Mates at Telstra. The NBN has shown little effort to negotiate purchases of Telstra assets, instead paying Telstra $1.6 billion to upgrade its existing networks. NBN also paid Optus $800 million simply to turn off its coaxial fibre network. There seems to be no desire to invoke compulsory acquisition powers to gain ownership of remaining Telstra networks, and no desire to take the ideal route of ignoring its pleading entirely and simply build a competitor network. Because of these deals, the NBN has so far cost tens of billions of dollars and is unfortunately a sign of how difficult it is to break down the various Games even when there is a strong political will to do so. A good plan can come unstuck when repeated minor changes that solve temporary political issues result in undermining the entire endeavour.

In the airline industry, individual airports for decades made 'abnormally high' profits from parking rights, office spaces and selling off their land, all of which was given to them by government and with governments picking up the bills for roads, water and transportation to airports (Productivity Commission, 2011).

In defence, the Australian government committed to buy dozens of submarines at hugely inflated prices, with no enemy in sight. Submarines are not defensive weapons, but offensive ones. It appears we are only buying them to please the Americans and keep a few marginal constituents happy, but the whole thing is so overpriced and over-hyped that we are clearly looking at a

James classic, costing the taxpayer potentially over $100 billion over the machines' useful lifetime. This is normal though: almost every country suffers huge wastes in its military budgets, probably resulting from the abuse of secrecy that is innate to defence.

Whatever corner of the economy in which you look, you will find a group of James and his Mates doing their best to subvert power to their own ends, with varying degrees of success.

12

Consequences of the Game of Mates

In all the sectors of the economy we have looked at, James cosies up to political power, where the juiciest grey gifts can be had. He forms his group of Mates, then together they implicitly, and cooperatively, abuse the power they hold within the institutions of our country, trading grey gifts amongst themselves for their joint benefit. James and his Mates are now often the politicians, as well as top bureaucrats, and the executives of Australia's biggest companies, sometimes even at the same time. The Game of Mates is now so widespread in Australia that it is itself a sector. Aspiring Jameses are queuing up in our capital cities with plans to defraud the population.

The Game is having surprising consequences for Australian culture. The full extent is hard to see, and impossible to prove, because cultures change for many reasons and the Game is only one of them. Still, we want to outline the direction in which we think the Game is pushing Australian culture, even if that involves more than a dash of speculation.

For instance, because of our close experience for many years investigating the Game in Queensland, we believe Queensland politics is best thought of as the competition between gangs of property developers, some aligned with one major party, some aligned with both. No doubt other states are similar, yet we have not had the hands-on experience elsewhere to see just how deeply this captures the underlying politics of those states.

Because the Game is so entrenched in both main political parties, losing an election is now merely the end of the immediate political career and the start of a lobbying career. Losing an election simply presents politicians an opportune time to leave office and join the lobbying game, capitalising on their trust and reputation amongst the Mates. As long as their party has a reasonable chance to get into power in the future, all the main groups of Jameses in the various sectors will need lobbyists that come from either party to ensure their Game continues. This is now just as true at the federal level as it is at the state level. The only difference is that the Game at the state level is more concentrated on decisions made at the state level, like property market decisions.

James's essential Game of developing his relationship network at the top of society starts very early in life. James goes to schools where he meets his future conspirators. Everyone who wants their children to be another James is trying to get their children into the schools where this networking happens. This has led to the peculiar phenomenon of a proliferation of private schools that do not even attempt to compete on academic merit, as they do in many other countries. Rather, they compete in sports, brand names, identity-building and prestige. The onlookers know exactly what these buzzwords mean, as they are a covert signal telling of the school's ability to build powerful relationship networks. Some 34 per cent of children now attend private schools, costing their parents tens of thousands of dollars per child per year, whilst academically oriented public schools cost very little. The additional expenses are a cost of the Game of Mates; one that society would not incur if there was no Game.

Not only that, James has ensured that by 2015 over 1000 private schools were getting more federal government funding per student than the average public school, further entrenching his head start in the networking game, and the disconnect between him and his Mates, and the many Sams and their Mates in the public at large (Jacks, 2015). Despite the popular Gonski needs-based funding reforms of 2017, per student public funding of private schools has continued to grow at a faster rate than public schools. We aren't the only ones pointing out the role James plays in the area of school funding. 'The wealthy private schools, with their secret lobbying and political clout, are obstacles to needs-based funding, which is necessary for both equity and efficiency reasons' (Menadue, 2015).

Networking not only occurs in private secondary schools, it is a feature of life at universities, business organisations, professional associations and within political parties.

Not all networking is a bad thing. Networking is also a means of matching employees and employers, and for learning about optimal ways of adopting new technology. It is when networking is used to defraud the many for the benefit of the few—when the groups that form control grey gifts that cost the rest of us—that it is unwanted. It is therefore very difficult to say how much of the networking activities in our economy should be counted as part of the Game, but the additional expenses on private schools seem wholly unnecessary as productive networking could equally happen in a cheaper school system.

Apart from affecting life in education, and determining much of the networking in our society, the Game of Mates also affects political culture. To be part of that Game is now the main reason to go into politics, to join unions and devote time in industry groups. As Menadue and Keating already noticed in their analysis back in 2015, government ministries have become politicised and infiltrated by lobbyists; playing the Game is no longer a fringe activity within political parties, but rather it is the main thing those parties do, diverting political discussion, debate and energy, away from their core job of improving our laws and institutions (Menadue and Keating, 2015). And the situation has deteriorated since then.

Consider how the Game of Mates is now dominant in political parties. Party elders, primarily former politicians and professional fixers, are the ones organising the Game of Mates inside their parties. They will network with the promising young politicians, ensuring that particularly honest and competent politicians are kicked out of the party before they can become too powerful. They organise the tribes within political parties, appointing the new generation of Jameses to key positions of influence, of course in return for lending a willing ear to the interests of the former politicians, whether they are now directors of superannuation firms, directors of property development firms, or executives at universities or mining companies.

It is an open question whether young politicians know what they are letting themselves in for when they enter politics and run for political parties. We think the majority of them are probably naive at the outset and have no idea what politics is truly like. They start out with convictions, plans and hopes, and the good ones will simply often quit when they realise they are not wanted by their own party elders and backers.

An example of the political machine taking control can be seen in the actions of Rob Pyne, elected in 2015 as the member of parliament in Queensland for the Labor party in Cairns following a career as a local councillor. He started tabling instances of corruption at the local government level from all over Queensland in late 2015. Instead of praising him and investigating the material he tabled, the party hierarchy reacted by forcing him out of the party, dismissing any evidence out of hand, and conducting a media campaign against him, as other MPs and the party organisation closed ranks against him (Robertson, 2016). This tells you about the internal organisation of the Labor party in Queensland, as well as the willingness of the other politicians in the Game to go along with this blatant attempt to silence a critic.

The case of Rob Pyne also shows how the two major parties cooperate with each other when their joint interest, which is the continuation of the Game, is threatened. Rob Pyne's constituency was strategically split by the 2017 redistribution of electoral areas, a decision made by an apparently non-partisan commission. After the change, Rob no longer lived in his own electorate.

Since the support for a 'maverick' is invariably local, this meant Rob Pyne had to choose at the next election which of the new electoral areas to stand for. Unsurprisingly, Rob Pyne narrowly lost the 2017 Queensland parliament election. His example can now be used as a warning to other would-be mavericks inside both major parties that they will be gotten rid of one way or another if they threaten the Game.

Some politicians will get into politics knowing full well what they are entering, perchance already having a commercial agenda to pursue. Many will start out with some degree of public spirit, then be seduced, for the attentions of the party elders and commercial backers are flattering and only slowly become a game of 'I scratch your back; you scratch mine', with ever greater favours being exchanged. These politicians simply surround themselves with excuses and rationalisations.

The poisoned political culture also permeates the state apparatus. Political masters need to present a story of their agenda to the population, all the while doing the bidding of James, who holds the threat of a well-versed media storm if he does not get what he wants. To appease James, politicians will even directly invite James to dictate policy, such as by inviting him to the top meetings inside the ministries and government institutions, to the despair of the good civil servants there. The policies that are pre-cooked by his think tanks get adopted by ministries, which have seen their own ability to resist James's Game diminish over time.

Surely not, you might say. But alas, surely yes. It is possible, for instance, to buy time with the prime minister and state premiers. Many former ministers at the state and federal level are now professional lobbyists. Paul Keating is a darling of the superannuation industry. Christopher Pyne is a darling of the defence industry. Some insiders have gone public over the astonishing degree to which legislation is drafted by James and his Mates, such as the involvement of mining lobbyist James Mackay in writing Queensland environmental legislation for the Liberal National Party government in 2012 (Solomons and Willacy, 2014).

Let us give a personal example from our own work on property market rorts in Queensland. We tried to do the right thing and informed the Queensland minister of planning, Jackie Trad, about the favouritism to well-connected developers that we found in our research. Guess what? After a seven-month delay, when the media storm over our findings had died down, we received a letter from the minister's chief of staff, Matthew Collins. When not a political operative, he earned his crust as a property consultant. His opinion of our work was that nothing untoward was happening, because in his mind it was 'the nature of the industry' for government to routinely favour well-connected developers. While we don't doubt he acted in that role with genuinely good intentions, the very nature of the Game means that having him and his Mates in the planning ministry in Queensland is little better than having wolves guarding the sheep.

The takeover of state institutions by the Game of Mates is blatant in many sectors. What can be said for property can be said for infrastructure, mining, banking, defence, and many other sectors, both in the Commonwealth and across the states.

Supposedly independent institutions and ministries are now doing the bidding of the few.

Where are the limits you might think. How bad can it get?

Despite the widespread Game of Mates, Australia's democracy functions relatively well. Everyone must vote; there is some degree of genuine political competition; and anything that is too obviously self-serving is punished. This limits the Game to being nonviolent and indirect, run not through theft and bribery, but relying on a long-term indirect and implicit Game of Mates that capitalises on the complexity of many laws, along with widespread myths, to fly under the radar.

The need to fly under the radar gives James an incentive to encourage political apathy, distrust and a general lack of interest in good journalism and political analysis. The more tuned out the general population, the more that James can get away with his Game before voters notice. James is all in favour of distractions for the population, whether they are sports events, ideologies that justify his grabbing, a public health emergency like Covid or salacious gossip about party intrigues. Anything to prevent the population from noticing they are robbed in broad daylight.

What do people notice who have no interest in politics and news? What is the limit to how much they can be abused?

The one thing they will notice is whether their life is getting worse. Marked reductions in wellbeing will not escape Sam's attention, no matter how absorbed they might be in their own daily life. As we saw, it took a depression in the 1890s to generate a wave of reforms in the early 1900s that shared Australia's wealth more widely.

The level of economic growth therefore limits what James and his Mates can steal. He and his Mates cannot easily steal large parts of the economic wealth that the rest of the population already has, for that would be noticed and strongly resisted. But if the economy is growing, he can take for himself the majority of the growth, leaving Sam's share growing ever so slightly by comparison.

Since the economy of Australia is now around two-and-a-half times larger per capita than in 1975, if James has captured all of the growth since then, he would have captured 60 per cent of the current economy. As we will calculate later on, we think he and his Mates have done a bloody good job of capturing most of it, leaving the rest not much better off than they were in the 1970s.

One of the hidden effects, which you could also see as a positive one, relates to immigration to Australia. Net immigration to Australia was around 200,000 people per year until the abrupt stop in 2020 due to Covid. For a whole decade before 2020, immigration was 1 per cent of the current population, which is more than double the immigration rate of other developed countries. Australian immigration is peculiar in that apart from a few humanitarian cases and family-related immigrants, we only let in well-trained and wealthy people, often as students or as young professionals.

Consider the politics of this. Who benefits the most from additional skilled workers? Other workers who would have to compete for jobs and already live here? Or James and his Mates, the bosses and owners in monopolised sectors of the economy, who benefit from selling new apartments, pharmaceuticals, superannuation funds and new mortgages? Of course, it is James. New immigrants do not compete in his Game. New immigrants do not have political networks. They did not go to school here, nor will their families have political networks already in this country. They simply come to swell the numbers of those James can rob. We believe it is James's political support that has led to massive immigration to Australia in recent decades.

This is not some crazy view. If you think it is, you should reflect on just how successful James's myth-making has been. Even the bland, boring and politically conservative Productivity Commission, after considering the matter, came down on our side: 'the distribution of these benefits varies across the population, with gains mostly accrued to the skilled migrants and capital owners. The incomes of existing resident workers grow more slowly than would otherwise be the case' (Productivity Commission, 2006).

And if you think that immigration is solving population ageing and making it easy to support the retirement of baby boomers, you would be wrong too. It is another myth. After all, immigrants age at the same rate as the rest of us. Again, this is well known. The Productivity Commission back in 2005 investigated the economic ramifications of population ageing and concluded that 'Despite popular thinking to the contrary, immigration policy is also not a feasible countermeasure' (Productivity Commission, 2005).

The economic effect of high immigration is not all bad. Depending on the composition of immigrants, it can contribute to creating a diverse population of well-educated and well-adapted new citizens. Current workers would normally oppose a massive influx of new immigrants, yet the political clout of James and his Mates kept the inflow coming. Australia's average population growth since 2007 has been around 1.6 per cent, which is 0.5 percentage points higher than pro-immigration Canada. If instead of being the immigration world leader, Australia had matched second-place Canada's level of immigration over the previous decade, there would have been 1.3 million fewer people in Australia in 2017.

Despite Australia's record high levels of immigration, immigrants themselves integrate surprisingly well, much better than in many countries, and many locals end up marrying them. Rapid immigration and population growth stimulate overall economic growth, which is the condition in which James and his Mates thrive, as they are able to skim off most of these gains.

This concentration of wealth and power arising as a consequence of the Game is starkly seen in Australia's corporate landscape. Former ACCC chairman Rod Sims noted in a speech just how much of the economy is being controlled by just a few top companies (Sims, 2016). He presented data showing that the total revenue of the top 100 companies in Australia increased from 15 to 47 per cent of GDP between 1993 and 2015: an astounding concentration of power over the economic activities of the country, which of course comes with political power as well.

The Game of Mates underpins this pattern of corporate concentration in Australia. Evidence of this can be seen in the networks of cross-directorships, whereby James and his Mates appoint each other to their boards of directors, increasing their ability to cooperate and repay favours amongst the big end of town, excluding others. Sociologists have been mapping the degree of interconnectedness between company directors, finding a steady increase since the 1970s, particularly for the larger companies in banking and finance, which Rod Sims noted are beginning to dominate economic activity, and which we have identified as industries controlled by James at enormous cost to the rest of us (Alexander, 2003; Etheridge, 2012). The role of company directors is now more about relationship-building than about their expertise in making their products and running their business.

A very pernicious effect of the Game of Mates has been on the ideology of the country. In the 1970s, Australia was a country with a strong egalitarian ethos that did not suffer inequality or 'tall poppies'.

That has almost entirely gone out of the window. Tall poppies now abound, and the population is being taught to look up to them. There are First Class lounges at the airports, elite clubs in the major cities, special holiday resorts for the super-rich, magazines where the super-rich can talk about how marvellous it is to have servants to do their laundry, and a pervasive 'compliance and leadership' culture that children are taught at school from a very young age. The 'compliance' is with whatever the Jameses of this world want from them, and 'leadership' is all about becoming the next James.

Slowly the next generation of Australians is being taught to admire James, not question his authority or his gains, and to meekly play along in the hope of picking up a crumb here or there. The generation of sheep is at school right now. The maverick battlers of previous generations, with stories of Ned Kelly and the Eureka Stockade, almost do not exist any more. James is telling their children to be quiet and to hope that he might make a place for them at his table, meanwhile telling them to accept their second-place lot in life.

In short, Australia has become a class society, with an elite who robs the rest who are scrambling to salvage some self-esteem by secretly hoping to join that elite. The pathetic kowtowing to wealth that is so typical of class societies is replacing the proud culture Australia had just decades ago, where tall poppies were cut to size. The tall poppies have had their revenge.

13
How Much Does the Game Bleed You?

Let us tally up what we think the Game roughly costs you in the sectors we have looked at, where we have made comparisons between Australia's current situation and world's best practice in that sector, wherever that happens to be.

New housing
James takes an estimated 70 per cent of the gains from rezoning and other planning decisions. Compared to best practice in our own backyard, the ACT, we are handing over $19 billion to James each year.

Transportation infrastructure
For every dollar spent on infrastructure, Sam gets an estimated 50 per cent less economic benefit because James and his Mates maximise their value from owning new roads, not the value of the road network to the population, so we end up with the

wrong new roads built that don't improve the overall transport network as much as others.

Superannuation

James gobbles up an estimated 27 per cent of Sam's super-annuation through his exorbitant annual fees, control of default funds and power to invest superannuation funds on projects with his Mates. This adds up to around $30 billion of extra fees a year, not to mention the $36 billion in tax breaks on the wealthiest superannuation funds, which are those of James and his Mates.

Mining

In the mining sector, James takes from Sam around 48 per cent of the profits in the resources sector, which could be shared under a Norwegian tax scheme. That was around $20 billion per year over the past decade. In addition, there are $36 billion of grey gifts in the form of subsidised infrastructure and unfunded environmental damage that Sam will pay for in the future.

Banking

Sam pays up to 80 per cent more over their lifetime on the cost of a mortgage to buy a house and for small business loans. Because James has protected his banking monopoly and infil-trated all corners of the financial regulatory system, he gains around $20 billion per year in extra profits from owning and running the banks.

Taxes

Multinational tax avoidance and tax lurks for the wealthy, such as family trusts, removed inheritance taxes and discounted capital gains taxes means that Sam pays an estimated 23 per cent extra in federal income taxes alone. That's a $70 billion per year gift to James and his Mates.

Pharmacies, medicines and health

Sam pays around twice as much for prescription medication than our counterparts in New Zealand, thanks to a system that looks after the interests of James and his Mates in the pharmaceuticals industry. This is at least a $1.3 billion yearly gift to James, possibly as much as $10 billion if we accept the statement that Australian patients would be no worse off if we adopted the same list of medicines as used in New Zealand and that we hence use a lot of expensive medicines we simply should not have. At the pharmacy, Sam pays at least 10 per cent more because of the grey gifts to James in that sector, which has a protected monopoly on retailing. And in the private insurance market, public subsidies in the form of tax rebates amount to a $3 billion gift each year.

Higher education

Because James and his Mates have control of the university sector, Sam pays about double what they should because of the additional staff overhead and exorbitant salaries of the senior managers at universities.

Other

In agriculture, Sam hands James billions in drought assistance and farm tax breaks. Telecommunications costs are hard to judge, but we have seen many billions wasted to support the financial interests of James in this sector too. And there is always defence, where billions of dollars of waste come with the territory, no matter which country you are in.

For decades, taxis cost an estimated 16 per cent more, and food prices were 13 per cent higher than they could have been, while James held sway in those sectors. The competition from outsiders to James's Game in these sectors clawed back billions for Sam. Though the fight was at many times dirty, it is a sign that things can change when there is enough pressure from outsiders to the Game.

We have not looked in detail at all sectors of the Australian economy, simply concentrating on the main ones to make clear that James is running the show just about everywhere at this moment. He particularly dominates those uncompetitive areas where the inherent right of the public to such things as minerals and property rights or the money system conflicts with private company interests in those areas.

To paint the overall picture of the theft from Sam in the areas we have looked at, we can try to envisage how much of the potential income streams that could go to Sam are siphoned off by James, and then to look at the expenditure side and see how much more Sam pays for goods and services because James is taking a cut there too. In Figure 12 we show just how much of a financial and economic cut James is taking from Sam's life.

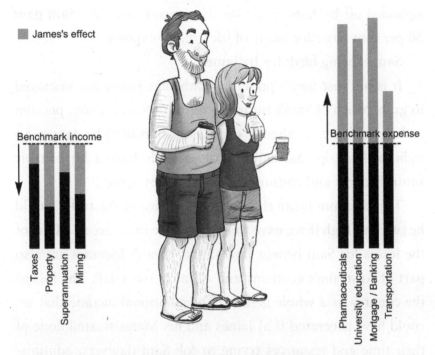

Figure 12: **Sam getting fleeced making an income and spending it**

The grey shading on the left shows the proportion of the incomes in that industry that Sam misses out on compared to our world's best benchmarks, giving Sam less in the back pocket. On the right are the extra costs on Sam's expenditure in other industries where James is taking a cut—from Sam's mortgage, education and medicines and in the costs of transportation.

Combining the effects of the educed share of wealth on Sam's income, and increased costs, Sam's real economic wellbeing appears to be around half of what it would be in our benchmark world without James and his Mates. In other words, we estimate that James robs you of nearly half of your wealth. Of the income that should reach Sam, around 30 per cent is siphoned off by James, and on the expenditure side, Sam pays 50 per cent more for many of life's major expenses.

Sam is being bled dry by James.

It is not just Sam's present wealth that James has managed to grab. Much of Sam's future, in terms of Sam's house, pension and health care, is already owned or controlled by James. So tight is this grip that children too already have a lot of their future income and consumption usurped by James.

This does not mean that the total income of Australia would be twice as high if we went to best practice in all areas. Many of the losses for Sam benefit James, and James's incomes are also part of Australia's economy and count in our GDP. The loss to the country as a whole is rather the additional income that we could have generated if a) James and his Mates wasted none of their time and resources trying to rob Sam (lawyers, administrators, tax consultants, bogus journalists, lobbyists), and instead James's resources were devoted to productive activities, and b) more economically beneficial investments were undertaken, instead of the sub-optimal ones that allowed James to get a larger share (such as the case of PPP transport projects).

It is also worth pointing out that in reality the situation is far more complex than a clear divide between James and Sam. A person who is a Sam in one part of the economy may be a James in another part. The 4000 pharmacy owners who are the Jameses in their sector, for instance, are the Sams when it comes to paying the price for James's control over grey gifts in transport investment or in superannuation. So too for the bank director who is fleeced by the pharmacists and for his share of rezoning gains. The Sam of our story who loses half their wealth is the Australian who does not benefit from any of these Games; they are outside all the elites that play the Game.

As you might have noticed, in each chapter we compared the existing situation with some notion of the 'best possible outcome' that was achievable. For these best possible outcomes in each sector we looked around the world for information, or we looked in different states in Australia over time.

For infrastructure, we needed to look no further than Australia in the 1970s for a system that was close to best practice. For property development and planning, we used the ACT as the example of best practice. For mining taxation, we looked to Norway. When it came to superannuation, we looked to Denmark. For health, we had to look no further than New Zealand. Only when it came to banking did we have to consider systems that have not yet been tested in the modern era but that have historical examples (in Australia in the middle of the twentieth century) and that are being proposed again in the United Kingdom and elsewhere.

What this means is that there is no country that has an optimal system in every sector. We held up Denmark as a country that has a good system for superannuation, but we didn't tell you that it has its own severe problems in property development. We held up New Zealand as a good place in terms of the health system but neglected to mention they suffer just as badly from Jameses in property development and in banking. Thus, we cannot say that life on average is better in many other countries at all. Rather, life is better in some sectors in other countries, though also often even worse in other sectors in those countries.

The costs of the Game are then what we think the costs are relative to the best country that Australia could be if we went to best practice in each sector, something that no country has yet achieved. We remain positive that a highly functioning wealthy, well-educated, cooperative democracy like Australia can be far closer to our benchmark in many areas if Sam can organise the political pressure to seek it.

14
Rise up, Sam

We have seen the Game of Mates play out in the major sectors of the Australian economy. We have also teased out the four main ingredients of the Game of Mates. And we have seen what James's Game of Mates costs Sam and Sam's family over their lifetimes.

Yet it is worth reiterating that the Game of Mates is not new. It is an age-old game. A dance for power. Special interests will always emerge and try to co-opt those in power, but societies do advance. They reform, such as in the Cromwell reforms of the seventeenth century in Britain or in the reform era under Bob Hawke in Australia.[37] Effective modern reforms can be done without bloodshed when there is enough political organisation and pressure delivered to James.

It is also worth warning against the temptation to fall into the trap of believing that the types of favouritism occurring in the Game happens because James and his Mates are bad, or selfish, people. No. They are normal people who succumb to the temptation of looking after those closest to them at the expense of others. The Game is a very pro-social one. Calling for 'better people' in government or in the various roles in each sector that drive the Game is a waste of time. Like we saw in our experiments, even the most honest people will be tempted into the Game, justify it to themselves and feel good about it. Because of this, we must consider how to set up systems that take away many of the necessary ingredients for the Game to occur. And as you would have noticed, being a bad person is not one of the ingredients.

So how can Sam reclaim their rights and take a share of the economic pie that James and his Mates are taking for themselves? We will not go into enormous detail of what we think would work in each sector and the specific political and legal hurdles, because we have made suggestions to that effect in earlier chapters. We instead sketch out the principles of good solutions in any sector.

Reclaim the value of grey gifts for the public

In each individual sector, the main way to reduce the cost of the Game is to reclaim the value granted by the public through its creation of favourable regulations for private companies. We have seen that the size of the giveaway to James and his Mates is enormous—a complete waste of resources from the perspective of the government and of Sam. Yet much of the mythology that helps to conceal the true motives of the Game of Mates relies on the idea that government must live within its means (in the case of PPP projects), or that taxing and charging particular groups of Jameses for their rights will send them packing, destroying the industry entirely (such as in mining and property).

The conflict between the myth that governments must live frugally and the reality that governments are giving away favours worth tens of billions of dollars a year to the same Mates propagating this myth can be leveraged to the advantage of Sam. Sam can use James's myth against him, insisting that governments reclaim all of the public value that it gives (and has given) to James. Each level of government can tax, or sell, the value of the grey gifts.

Increasing competition, often by creating a public competitor company, will ensure that any collusion amongst private companies is limited to the degree to which the public company can undercut the inefficiencies and higher prices arising from collusion. In establishing public competitors, such as in banking, universities and land development, expertise should be drawn from international sources where possible to avoid James and his Mates infiltrating that new organisation as well.

James only has two responses to new public competition. First, resist it and ensure anyone who takes up a job in new government entities is excluded from the Game of Mates, removing their ability to reclaim future favours, and to attack them in the press to unsettle the would-be competitor. The second option is to capture the new public organisation by immediately stacking it with Mates. In a political environment that had the incentive to create such an organisation, this second option, we hope, would be very difficult to implement. We can therefore expect a massive media attack.

Any effective change will engender a massive backlash from James, and we have seen such attacks before. The mining industry saw off the attempt by the 2010 Labor government to tax the grey gifts they had been given. No less fury should be expected next time around.

In principle, one could reclaim the grey gifts already stolen. One could tax the value given in the past with new tax laws. This may sound strange because it is not possible to make something a crime after the fact, but when it comes to taxation that is not true; all taxes on wealth are essentially taxing activity of the past as wealth is accumulated in the past. So one can set up a new tax that syphons off a high percentage of the profits made by the Games of Mates played in the last 30 years. Perhaps a package of laws can help find those gifts, for instance by offering a generous 'finder's fee' (a bounty) for anyone who can prove there was a particular gift given. A 5 per cent finder's fee on deals worth billions will test the loyalty of Mates, and we shall see whether hordes of Jameses fall over themselves to dob each other in. While in practice this approach is likely to be difficult to apply broadly, there may be sectors of the economy and public service where it can first be narrowly applied as a policy experiment. Targeting the wealth earned by activities deemed corrupt in hindsight is hence one way for the public to seek justice and to undo the huge increase in inequality of the last 30 years.

Outside these core ways to reclaim the value of grey gifts, the public could insist that anyone employed by the public sector, or a sector that lives mainly off government contracts (like hospitals and universities), cannot have a total personal income higher than some maximum, such as the income of the prime minister.[37] Germany and the Netherlands adopted such a rule in the hope of containing the honey pots within the public sector itself.[38] It limits the gains available to people managing public institutions, such as hospitals and universities, who can be appointed on political whims and because of their relationships and bias towards the interests of James and his Mates.

Former CEO of the government-owned Australia Post, Ahmed Fahour, for example, was paid a salary and bonus of over $5 million in 2016, an astonishing figure that was kept secret for years and when discovered led to his immediate resignation.

What we should not do is pretend that government regulators are going to be able to properly police the actions of wealthy, powerful and well-connected firms from the outside via their weak regulatory bodies. More regulations that are difficult to enforce, and simply add discretion and complexity, almost always play into James's hands.

This is highly relevant to the trend towards PPPs and privatisation of public organisations. If governments believe they are unable to efficiently construct school buildings, hospitals, roads or powerlines through their own departments or government-owned companies, what magical skills do they believe they possess in order to effectively negotiate with, and regulate, the powerful private interests they are selling these assets to?

The idea of having a public competitor is to limit what the private sector monopolists can get away with when they are difficult to regulate directly. When you hear that an industry controlled by James and his Mates is willing to negotiate 'regulatory reforms', you know they are seeking to further entrench their position with regulations that suit them, and that will protect them from new competition, public or otherwise.

Disrupt James's coordination

In the administrative sphere, there are many improvements we think are worthwhile. One possible reform is to implement a rotation system that makes systematic use of a pool of foreign experts who fly in to make key decisions on discretionary government decisions. With a group of other comparable countries, we could simply set up pools of available experts that can be used to fly in and make decisions, with other countries borrowing our experts as well when needed. This should work well in areas like defence contracts (where discretionary purchases seem pretty much inevitable), and large infrastructure and rezoning decisions. A scheme of having foreign experts make decisions to ensure impartiality of those decisions is exactly what happens with the refereeing of international sports. Why can't it also be used for major technical, yet discretionary, public policy decisions? Such a change could be implemented very quickly and hence could be a first step towards deeper reform inside Australia.

A more ambitious improvement that uses the idea of rotation, or randomisation, and that we think has a good chance of working to protect us from the next wave of Jameses, is to strengthen the independence of government departments. One way is to have people at the top of government departments, the secretaries, or CEOs of statutory bodies, be appointed via a jury system, replacing the current situation where politicians and special interest groups are heavily involved in deciding on top positions in the civil service.

What we have in mind here is that juries made up of random members of the population, or from members of the whole public service, assemble just for the purpose of job appointments. One jury, one top position. What we have in mind is that there would be administrative support, such as by the current electoral commissions, for assembling and aiding juries. Top positions that needed to be filled would be advertised beforehand with no major limits on who could apply. The juries of, say, ten to twenty random people, would make their own rules about minimum eligibility requirements and what kind of person they wanted for a top job. They would have the power to appoint anyone they wanted, including from amongst those who did not apply. Over time, such juries could be assisted by people who have gone through appointment juries and thus know about how to deliberate constructively, recognise attempts at manipulation, and so on. It would be a civic duty to be part of a jury when randomly chosen, just as is now the case with juries on criminal trials.

Citizen juries would make hundreds of appointments each year, including the heads of all major government departments and institutions, but also all universities, hospitals, state media and statistical agencies. This would involve thousands of members of the public who would be taken seriously as citizens since they then suddenly have something of real importance to decide.

The immediate advantage we expect from appointments by citizen juries is that James is kept away from the appointments: the political networks around top positions would be neutered at a stroke. Whomever a jury appoints is very unlikely to be the person that James would have most wanted to be there.

A longer term advantage is that the population is more involved in actual decision making. Serving on appointment juries would be a democratic civic duty, which is how the first democracy in ancient Athens functioned: the old Athenians distrusted professional politicians because they thought they would inevitably turn into crooks. In ancient Athens random citizens were appointed to be the top decision makers. We think that in current times one needs specialists to run departments and many institutions like statistical agencies and media companies, so we don't advocate random citizens to be appointed as directors, but we do think random citizens should do the choosing. That is how the city of Venice for some time chose its leader, the Doge of Venice: randomly chosen committees of (rich) citizens chose the Doge, a system designed to prevent takeover by small clans.

Our proposal uses the key strength of the jury system to be able to read the character of a person by their history and to judge on whether they have behaved honourably in the past or not, which works reasonably well in criminal courts.[39] Juries who make a very particular decision form a very small target for James since they only exist for a few weeks and make decisions that each on their own are not that important. Manipulating short-lived juries is rather tough.

We think such a system would help to select knowledgeable and public-spirited civil servants, or outsiders, to get the top jobs in ministries, and that it would help to limit the ability of special interest groups to get someone favourable to their cause into powerful positions in the government. Instead of a revolving door of insiders, we would see greater rotation of outsiders into powerful government positions with access to grey gifts. It would thus add to the independence of the civil service and erect another barrier to James. We think this idea can also be extended to the top of semi-private companies that produce key public goods, like media: one could insist that the top manager of every large media company operating in Australia is to be appointed by a jury of Australian citizens. The reason to 'interfere' in a private company in this way is that media inevitably interferes with how the population views itself and gets exposed to politics, making it essential to have a system that avoids private parties from manipulating public opinion for private gain.

A related idea is to extend the jury idea to a citizen parliament. Queensland, for example, scrapped its upper house in the 1920s. A policy experiment worth trying is to reinstate it as a parliament of randomly chosen citizens, and a share of the group replaced every four years. This would create direct oversight of decisions by a group of people completely outside the various Games at play.

The current politicians and other sets of Jameses will invoke many myths against these proposals if they were to become widely debated. They will point out that experiments with powerless citizen assemblies have proven them to be powerless (which is true, but says nothing about juries and parliaments that do have real power). They will pretend that random citizens cannot be trusted to know who should lead important agencies, even though they are trusted in our system to appoint the top politicians. They will pretend that it would be too costly or too difficult to run a citizen jury or citizen assembly system, even though juries and assemblies have been around for centuries. We are sure they will come up with other innovative myths when their Game is threatened.

A different line of thinking pertains to current lobbying rules. We can extend cooling-off periods for politicians and regulators that restrict them from working in the industry they previously controlled, which is standard professional practice for auditors and accountants.

Already there are minimum periods between the political career of a politician and the moment they can lobby professionally. But the current rules are extremely narrow. In Queensland for example, the rules apply only to elected politicians and limited senior staff. They only apply to jobs as professional lobbyists. This excludes working directly inside companies they previously regulated and working for think tanks and professional bodies whose primary function is to lobby, but who are not strictly defined as professional lobbyists. Reforming this will make it a bit harder for James to reward the politicians for the favours they have done him.

We can of course directly set up institutions with a mandate to investigate favour exchanges and to report on it in the open. A statutory body could be charged with keeping tabs on the major grey gifts given to private interests by the political and administrative systems in our country and suggesting improvements where James has managed to get his foot in the door. To a large extent, this role is already taken up by journalists and watchdogs, including the Productivity Commission, the RBA, the ACCC and others, so this would not require all that much more than picking an institution already doing some of this and making it an official mandate. The public broadcaster can also be strengthened in its ability to do investigative journalism, which would be a boon for Sam.

Such activities are usually beyond the scope of the various state anti-corruption agencies. Most of these are limited to investigating detailed complaints that are made to them; many cannot trigger their own investigations, and they are usually only able to seek out wrongdoing where there is direct evidence of corrupt acts. These agencies are of course necessary to catch the worst cases of cronyism, fraud, bribery and corruption, and they have had some success.

Unfortunately, this means these anti-corruption agencies are often political targets. In 2021, the South Australian parliament passed legislation to reduce the powers of its anti-corruption agency so that it could no longer investigate the 'weaker' charges of maladministration and misconduct. After its investigations into council corruption in 2017, the Queensland anti-corruption commission became the target of political pressure. Because some of the cases brought to court did not result in convictions due to a lack of evidence, the watchdog was accused of overstepping its mandate and further reduction in its powers is likely.

The same problem will show up for any new independent anti-corruption body, such as a new federal anti-corruption body. Whilst many commentators expect a new body to solve most problems in one stroke, we think this is unlikely. Just think: who would appoint the head of a federal anti-corruption body in the current situation? Who would write its terms of reference and thus the scope of what they investigate? Who would decide on the changes to the annual budget, changes in what is deemed illegal and corrupt? There is just one answer to each of these questions: James. While we know such an agency can be effective at catching the most egregious cases of bribery, extortion and abuses of power, we fear that in a political environment where state anti-corruption commissions are being neutered that its scope will be limited.

Even with perfectly operating anti-corruption institutions, a major underlying issue is that the many billions of dollars of costly favouritism from the Game of Mates most often occurs without direct corrupt acts at all. James and his Mates don't need to hide from the laws they have themselves written. The key to any anti-corruption system is to make sure laws are written so that doing high-value favours is a criminal act.

Many reformers advocate more transparency about decisions to quell political favouritism. The idea is that if favours can be seen by the public, they can be stopped. But as we have detailed, many of the favours are in fact perfectly visible if you know where to look. The degree of transparency we already have does not seem to have helped, and it is hard to see how simply adding to the body of available information is going to tip the balance and create effective change by itself.

In fact, calls for transparency are very easily corrupted by James in his interests. Ask for transparency and you will get it, but not in a form that makes any sense.

For example, in 2019 laws were passed that created a unique identifier for individuals who are company directors—a director identification number. Ostensibly it is to keep track of directors who take control of 'phoenix' companies and improve enforcement of this already illegal practice. Sounds okay, no?

Yet the name, address and date and place of birth of all company directors are already recorded in ASIC's corporate database. This information is already sufficient to uniquely identify all company directors within seconds through an electronic database search. We have done this exercise before in our own research. It is not clear to us what is being achieved apart from appearing to 'do something' about transparency. If director ID numbers ultimately replace personal information in public records, this would perversely result in less public transparency, not more.

We have reason to suspect this outcome. A myth we have seen used to push this approach is that directors might suffer from 'identity theft' if there is too much public information about them (Brogden, 2015; Robin, 2015). The lobby group for corporate directors, the Australian Institute of Company Directors, found that most directors were in favour of this additional director ID regulation, almost unanimously supporting it if it replaces all other personal information.

Hence, like we saw in superannuation, James loves additional regulation, even for transparency, because he will provide you transparency in exactly the form you do not want.

Don't misunderstand us. Transparency is good in principle, if it is timely and easy to grasp. But it does have to be used as a basis for real change and enforcement of existing rules, not coming instead of real change.

Sadly, public records of property and corporate ownership are dismally expensive and difficult to access. Family trusts and other legal structures allow James to conceal many of his financial relationships.[40] It is not clear to us why these public databases are not freely available. Indeed, we know radical transparency is possible. Every Norwegian's annual tax return is posted freely on the tax administration's website. The only catch, for fairness, is that each person can see the identity of others who have looked at their tax returns. We see a priority for transparency in property and corporate ownership records, as well as making public the contracts entered into by our public representatives, such as the currently secret PPP deals. The role of transparency in these areas will be to alert us where grey gifts have been given, and to help properly enforce existing laws.

Sometimes transparency can backfire. Imagine a committee of six people is deciding who should receive a lucrative new government construction contract. Should the identity of the committee be public knowledge? Or would a secret committee be better? A publicly known committee can be lobbied, whereas a confidential committee cannot be. This example shows that transparency can also play into the hands of James and his Mates, who can now more easily rely on public information to determine who is playing their Game, and who is not.

Referring back to our computer experiments on group favouritism discussed earlier, we had a variation where participants used iPads to take photos of themselves to identify each other. We found no reduction in favours given. When players could identify each other with photos, they used social cues, or signals, from the information in the photographs to form their alliance groups. Students who knew each other, such as in economics and business courses, found each other more easily to form their alliance. Transparency in isolation is therefore not effective at curtailing the Game of Mates. Only if transparency is a component of a larger effort to monitor and enforce systems that have less scope for favouritism and conflicts of interest is it likely to be in the interests of Sam.

Believing that technology can break James's Game is also a trap. In taxis and supermarkets, we saw that it wasn't the technology that disrupted James's Game, but a willingness to fight hard and long in complex regulatory debates, and even be willing to break laws that favour James in order to change them. Our examples from around the world of systems that kept James's Game at bay—in planning, transport, mining, banking, superannuation and education—all arose without the need for any new technology. James will also try to use new technology to defend his position, and the complexity it can create may also provide him new opportunities for grey gifts that are even more hidden from view.

Bust James's myths

The final avenue for Sam to combat James is to seek out alternative sources of news and information. Since James owns the mainstream media, the role of experts reaching out in online publications is perhaps a new alternative way to give Sam a peek behind the cloak of James's myths. An independent publicly funded news organisation also seems crucial to ensuring the media maintains a critical stance and calls out the blatant lies used to conceal the Game of Mates.

The risk, which has become a reality in some ways, is that when seeking out alternative sources of news Sam will find many bogus sources that are even less connected to reality than James's myths. The rising popularity of 'fake' news is simply the logical result of Sam waking up to the fact that most of the mainstream news was a regurgitation of James's myths anyway. Sam knows they are being conned but doesn't really know where to turn. Publicly minded journalists and media organisations must realise that there is a growing aversion to people who seem like they are part of the Game, meaning a growing distrust of experts and talking heads, and an appetite for leaders who are willing to challenge the status quo. Sam is no fool. Sam knows their own economic interests are not being looked after.

Disrupting myth propagation can also be done in various parts of education and employment. For instance, pharmaceutical companies currently pay universities for access to new medical students to indoctrinate them with their myths. Similarly, pharmaceutical companies have many thousands of infomercial workshops with doctors throughout the country to sell them on their myths. Some of these things can be disrupted relatively easily, just as advertising for gambling can be disrupted (though often is not).

It is also up to the research community, whose work we have drawn upon, to understand the Game of Mates, to realise they are part of a political Game. The facts are relatively clear and available for those who put in some effort. But the political battles rely on stories and fables that the general public will relate to. In that arena, the idea of a 'fair go' has taken a back seat to a set of myths that appeal to ideas of economic efficiency, but in reality, achieve the opposite.[41] Researchers and experts should challenge this at every turn, and create stories of their own that are more related to truth.

We should reiterate that the policy changes advocated in this book will not be easy to put on the political agenda, or to implement. James and his Mates will try to subvert every suggestion to suit them and strengthen their position, rather than weaken it, just as they already subvert the very words that describe what needs to be done to combat them (competitive, merit-based, excellent, ethical, value-based, evidence-driven, etc.). To rid ourselves of the current batch of Jameses will be a drawn-out affair that will take the sustained efforts of many of us.

Finally . . .

Many societies around the world, across many previous generations, have fought their Jameses and won. It is our turn now.

15
Covid Games

The world changed in early 2020 when Covid arrived on the global stage. While the media and policy reactions initially resembled the formation of a crowd—a mob-like state of mind with a sole object of focus where every action becomes viewed by how it related to that object of focus—it was quickly apparent that the door was opened for James to take advantage of the situation.

We do not want to dwell here on Covid and the policy reaction in 2020 and 2021, as one of us (Paul) has already written a book on it entitled *The Great Covid Panic*. But it is important to briefly note how James and his Mates quickly adapted to the new Game environment.

Enormous spending programs were set up in early 2020, purportedly to subsidise workers and businesses to stay at home rather than run around and be health risks to others. Those programs created a new suite of grey gifts regarding the decisions to be made about how to distribute funds to prop up spending in the economy. Record amounts were ultimately spent. The major new spending programs were JobSeeker, which boosted unemployment benefits, and JobKeeper, which provided a wage subsidy to businesses, totalling around $70 billion. The lesser-known Cashflow Boost scheme gave away another $34 billion in 2020 to 800,000 companies with turnover below $50 million per year, none of which needed to demonstrate hardship, and many of which saw massive profit boosts as spending was redirected to their businesses.

At first, few people saw how unnecessary these programs were. The myth-making about economic collapse and hardship provided ideal cover. Only Australian National University economists Rabee Tourky and Rohan Pitchford warned upfront that the design of JobKeeper would ultimately lead to a massive profit subsidy for a huge portion of the corporate recipients. Indeed, by mid-2021, it became apparent that the scheme gave billions to companies that saw increased turnover and profits, and a push was underway to force large publicly traded companies to repay these funds as a good-faith gesture. Only $200 million was repaid by the end of 2021.

A funny thing we noticed about the Cashflow Boost was how the recipients of it kept it so quiet. It attracted almost no public scrutiny compared to the other programs. No one who received it wanted to make a fuss for fear of losing their slice of the grey gift. Many recipients had probably seen the Jameses of their industry make easy wins before. It was their turn now. Yet when talking in private, many business owners were happy to make stunning admissions to us of how much obligation-free cash they got, and admit puzzlement as to why they got it.

There was also the rise of the safety theatre. With billions in government contracts up for grabs a new lucrative industry emerged for James to enter. The Wagners, a well-connected Toowoomba family, for example, secured a deal with the Queensland government to build a quarantine facility at their privately owned Wellcamp airport for an undisclosed public subsidy. The chances of this facility being used at all appeared low in early 2022, though Sam will pay for it regardless.

There have been thousands of government contracts up for grabs during the pandemic, ranging from bulk orders for masks, to refrigerator facilities for vaccines, to machines for dispensing hand-sanitiser, to mass regular testing, to closing down high-street shops in favour of online ones, to millions of pamphlets about the latest safety guidelines. We do not detail here the many scams James perpetrated on Sam in this period, though the reader is encouraged to read *The Great Covid Panic* for some of the juiciest stories pertaining to both Australia and the rest of the world.

What made the Covid era different from how the Game of Mates is usually played was the intense political dynamics. Those doubting official narratives or public spending were simply branded lunatics endangering the survival of the population. Such tough-guy politics worked well to deter any political competitors, and incumbent politicians, especially state premiers, seemed electorally untouchable. That made life even easier for James because scrutiny could be dismissed as 'endangering lives'. The old political motto that one should never let a good emergency go to waste was applied beautifully by James.

While the Covid era provides many examples of the lessons in this book, the main element it has added to the Game of Mates is an increased focus on stories around health and safety. A new group of powerful Jameses has arisen in the Covid era that has learnt how to fleece Sam by scaring them witless and convincing Sam that salvation lies in buying stuff from James and keeping their mouth covered.

Still, we think the Covid years in hindsight are likely to be seen as hastening the reform cycle in Australia. The isolation of Australia in 2020–2021 caused huge blows to many parts of the economy, particularly to all the easy money that flowed in before and that kept the place politically docile. Foreign tourists, foreign students and skilled immigrants stopped coming to Australia abruptly and completely in March 2020. The stop in skilled immigrants meant a sudden loss of human capital walking into the country that was paid for by other countries. It also meant that within Australia there was no influx of politically uncon-nected workers, yet private schools were still churning out new Jameses oriented towards competing for the productivity of the rest. So there was less easy money flowing in and more compe-tition for whatever remained.

Government debt also skyrocketed in the Covid period, projected to grow from 20 per cent of GDP in 2019 to 45 per cent before 2025. In previous periods, avoiding public debt was used as an excuse not to make public investments that were in Sam's interest. But when Covid hit, record debts were no longer seen as a concern, perhaps because James was a main beneficiary. Those debts will likely be repaid by reducing general public services (to Sam) in education and health. The chance that they will be repaid by more taxes on James is remote.

At the same time, the disruption to education and social life meant Australian children received fewer skills and were less socially active, both of which mean more disruptive young adults in the future.

In short, the Covid period led to a sudden impoverishment of Australians, combined with continuing drags on both the public purse and the mental health of Australians. Such downturns are exactly the period in which James's rigged Game becomes visible to Sam, since there is suddenly a lot less to go round. With no easy end to the rough times in sight, we think it quite probable that Sam is going to slowly awake from their long slumber and start to realise the full extent to which James has played them.

Economic loss from transport PPP projects

To quantify the scale of the economic loss associated with being a PPP project, we undertake the following analysis using data compiled by Elaurant and McDougall (2014) on 38 major infrastructure projects since 1991, and a separate dataset of benefit–cost ratios for Australian infrastructure projects (Productivity Commission, 2015), which we use to generate modelled benefit–cost ratios to apply to our main infrastructure project data. These represent a large cross-section of completed projects over a long period of time where their final success and use is known.

For the 38 projects, we first determine for each of them a modelled expected benefit–cost ratio if traffic forecasts were met for all $60.5 billion worth of spending. This involves fitting a model of benefit–cost ratios to project size from a secondary dataset to generate a coefficient of project size that could be applied to our 38 projects to determine a counter-factual level of expected benefits for each project, bc_i. A close-fitting model is double log, with an estimated ln(cost) coefficient of -0.24 ($p = 0.00$) for $N = 24$ projects undertaken between 2010 and 2013. Project size is the main source of variation in benefit–cost ratios, with large projects having much lower benefit–cost ratios. This means that choosing to build larger projects instead of numerous smaller projects reduces the net benefits from transport spending.

We then combine our expected benefit–cost ratios, bc_i, with project total cost, $cost_i$, a PPP dummy variable, PPP_i, and the traffic forecast error, α_i, that we have available for each project to get the economic loss due to being a PPP project for our dataset, compared to being a publicly funded project.

$$Dollar\ value\ loss = ln(bc_i \times PPP_i \times \alpha_i) -$$
$$ln(bc_i \times cost_i \times nonPPP_i \times \alpha_i)$$

Doing this gives a figure of $-\$28$ billion in 2015 dollar terms. This represents an estimate of lost economic output by choosing to invest $31 billion in PPP projects that did not have anywhere near the economic benefits they claimed to have.

We can also factor into this analysis another element of loss arising simply from the choice of project. Because benefit–cost ratios are tightly related to project size, and because the average PPP project was 34 per cent larger in costs terms than non-PPP projects, this itself is another element to consider. If we use the fitted benefit–cost ratio model to generate counter-factual expectations, the PPP projects are 1.9, and non-PPP are 2.0. We can now consider that if it were not for the existence of the PPP project arrangement, and the potential for grey gifts to be traded in such arrangements, that the same funds were instead spent on the mean size non-PPP projects, then an additional $4 billion in economic gains could be had. The total possible economic losses associated with PPP project arrangements for the projects in our database is estimated at $32 billion from a total of $31 billion on PPP projects, and $60 billion of overall spending.

Appendix
Historical snapshot of mining industry staff rotation

Federal ministers who became involved in mining after politics

John Anderson
- former deputy prime minister and leader of the National Party under the Howard government
- served as chair of coal-seam gas company Eastern Star Gas (acquired by Santos)

Craig Emerson
- minister for trade and competitiveness in the Rudd/Gillard governments
- economic consultant whose clients include AGL and Santos

Martin Ferguson
- minister for energy and resources in the Rudd/Gillard governments

- chair of Australian Petroleum Production and Exploration Association (APPEA) advisory board

Ian Macfarlane
- resources minister in the Howard government, industry minister in the Abbott government
- chief executive of the Queensland Resources Council

Mark Vaile
- former deputy prime minister and leader of Nationals under the Howard government
- chair of Whitehaven Coal

NSW Minerals Council staff

Ksenya Belooussova—digital communications manager, 2012–14
- media adviser at NSW Department of Premier and Cabinet 2014–15

Emma Browning—director, government relations
- media and policy adviser to 'NSW Shadow Minister'—1997–99

Brad Emery—director of communications
- press secretary to federal assistant treasurer, Peter Dutton MP 2004–07
- media adviser to Kerry Bartlett MP—1998–99

Stephen Galilee—CEO
- chief of staff of the former NSW treasurer, later NSW premier, Mike Baird

Lindsay Hermes—communications officer, 2010–13
- adviser to Ian Macfarlane, minister for industry and science 2013–15
- media adviser to the Liberal Party, 2013 federal election
- adviser to deputy leader of the Opposition, ACT government 2006–08

Scott Keenan—director, public affairs
- media adviser to NSW transport minister Michael Costa 2003–04

William Rollo—director, advocacy and engagement, 2020–21
- ministerial adviser to minister for resources, Matt Canavan 2016–17 and 2018–20, and to deputy prime minister Barnaby Joyce 2017–18

Sue-Ern Tan—deputy CEO, 2008–12
- senior policy adviser to Ian McDonald, Energy and Mining Office of the NSW minister for primary industries, minister for mineral resources, minister for energy, 2006–08

Minerals Council of Australia staff
Tania Constable—CEO
- chief adviser in the Personal and Retirement Income Division of Treasury

- adviser to the minister for industry on oil and gas regulation, exploration and development, and sustainable mining activities
- Australian Joint Commissioner and Sunrise Commissioner for Australia and Timor Leste

Victoria Jackson, executive director
- executive director, Energy, Department of Primary Industry and Resources, 2013–18

Ross Lambie—chief economist
- chief economist, Australian Chamber of Commerce and Industry, 2016–19
- chief economist, assistant secretary, Economics and Analysis Branch, Department of the Environment and Energy, 2016–19
- general manager, Resources and Energy Economics Branch, Department of Industry, Innovation and Science, 2015–16
- senior economist, manager, Gas Markets, Bureau of Resources and Energy Economics, Department of Resources, Energy and Tourism, 2013–14

Sid Marris—deputy CEO
- senior adviser, Energy, Climate Change, Resources and Northern Australia, Prime Minister Malcolm Turnbull, 2017–18

Chris McCombe—assistant director, environmental policy
- manager, Major Projects (Abandoned Mines Land Program) Queensland Mines and Energy, 2008–10

Chris Natt—training and education coordinator
- worked for NT minister for primary industries, minister for fisheries, minister for mines and energy, 2005–09

James Sorahan—executive director, director, taxation
- policy adviser, Martin Ferguson, 2010–13
- policy adviser, Chris Bowen, 2007–10
- policy analyst, Australian Treasury, 2005–07

Third-party mining lobbyists

Larry Anthony—founding director at SAS Group
- senior vice president federal Nationals, 2006–12

Liam Bathgate—director at Australian Public Affairs
- Lobbied for Shenua Watermark, Aston Resources (Maules Creek Coal Project) and Tenix Group
- chief of staff to Barry O'Farrell, 2007–08
- general secretary of NSW Nationals, 1992–97
- principal private secretary to Ian Sinclair MP (leader of federal Nationals), 1984–87
- press secretary to Doug Anthony MP (deputy prime minister and leader of federal Nationals), 1979–84

Brian Tyson—managing partner at Newgate Communications
- lobbied for Coalpac Pty Ltd
- press secretary NSW premier, Nick Greiner, and planning and energy minister, Robert Webster, 1987–95

Mathew Watson—managing director at Repute Communications
- lobbied for Bickham Coal and Port Waratah Coal Services
- senior communications manager (Cabinet/ministerial) in NSW government, 2002–04

Australian Petroleum Production and Exploration Association (APPEA) staff

Ryan Bondar—policy and government relations
- senior policy adviser to NSW leader of Opposition Barry O'Farrell, 2008–10
- research officer to Joe Hockey, 2003–04

Michael Bradley—director, external affairs
- ministerial adviser to Martin Ferguson, federal resources and energy minister, 2008–10

Sarah Browne, director of public affairs
- principal adviser—policy director, Office of the Premier, Victoria, 2014
- director of policy, Office of the Premier, WA, 2012–13; senior policy adviser, Office of the Leader of the Opposition, WA, 2001–05; research and policy adviser, Office of the Premier, WA, 1998–2001

Stedman Ellis—chief operating officer, Western Region, 2010–18
- deputy director general, WA Department of Mines and Petroleum, 2007–10

Paul Fennelly—chief operating officer, eastern Australia
- director-general (CEO) of Department of State Development, Trade and Innovation—General (Queensland)

Martin Ferguson—chair of APPEA advisory board
- minister for energy and resources in the Rudd/Gillard governments

Alexandra Gibson—policy director, NSW/Victoria
- adviser to Christopher Pyne, 2006–07

Damien Hills—national associate director, environment and safety
- senior policy adviser, Office of the Minister for Environment and Heritage (WA), 2001–02

Andrew McConville, CEO
- senior policy adviser, Victorian Department of Premier and Cabinet, 1994–96; Victorian Department of Treasury and Finance, 1996–98

Jason Medd, director Environment, Health and Safety
- principal policy officer, Department of Mines and Petroleum Western Australia, 2011–18

Kieran Murphy—director, external affairs, 2016–18
- communications director, Office of the Premier (WA), 2005–08
- adviser, Office of the Premier (WA), 2018

Simon Staples, director commercial

- director, energy and resources strategy, Australian Taxation Office, 2016–19
- policy adviser, corporate and international tax, Australian Taxation Office, 2014–16

Chris Ward—media manager, Eastern Australia

- principal media adviser to Queensland minister for transport, 2010–11
- press secretary to federal minister for consumer affairs and small business, 2008–10
- senior media adviser to the Queensland Treasurer, 2007–08
- senior media adviser to NSW attorney-general and minister for the environment, 2003–07

Adam Welch—senior policy adviser, Western Region

- senior policy officer/policy officer at Office of Energy (WA)
- executive office at Office of Energy (WA)

Ashley Wells, director, government relations

- senior adviser, Stephen Smith MP, 2004–08
- foreign affairs adviser, Kevin Rudd MP, shadow minister for foreign affairs, 2002–04

Claire Wilkinson, director Western Australia and South Australia

- senior media adviser to Ian Macfarlane, minister for industry, tourism and resources, 2007

Acknowledgements

In the good old days, the production of a book was measured in hectolitres of coffee, whole forests worth of early drafts, and angry looks of the significant other for being absent minded. Nowadays one has to add derelict websites, oodles of podcasts and tweets, warded-off DoD attacks, and a few angry letters by lawyers.

Yet, at a deeper level, books are measured in terms of love and companionship. Love for an ideal, the companions one tries to reach or help. It is a bit about self-indulgent rebelliousness too, of course. But let's focus on the good stuff.

In our case, the love and companions who spurred us on were the notion of a Fair Australia and a happy future for our children and close friends. So thanks to our children Robert, Carmen, Jasmine, Eli and Kai. We don't quite want to list all the friends we tried to reach or help for fear of missing out some, but you know who you are. Plenty of Bruces, Sams, and even the odd James.

Then of course we need to thank the co-producers: Richard Walsh, Elizabeth Weiss, Tom Bailey-Smith, Susan Keogh and Carissa Harris. You have been magnificent.

Lastly, of course, we have to thank those who put up with us: the significant others. Thanks Erika and Cathy.

References

Agriculture, Resources and Environment Committee. (2013). Mining and Other Legislation Amendment Bill 2012. Report No. 18. March 2013. Accessed on 20 January 2017 at www.parliament.qld.gov.au/documents/tableOffice/TabledPapers/2013/5413T2228.pdf

Akerman, P. (2016). Craig Thomson refuses to pay penalties, risks further action. *Australian.* 6 April 2016. Accessed on 20 January 2017 at www.theaustralian.com.au/national-affairs/industrial-relations/craig-thomson-refuses-to-pay-penalties-risks-further-action/news-story/b34e7b2beb661d664be0aceb0780571c

Alexander, M. (2003). Boardroom networks among Australian company directors, 1976 and 1996. *Journal of Sociology,* vol. 39, no. 3.

APRA. (2021). Quarterly private health insurance statistics. *Australian Prudential Regulation Authority.* Accessed on 10 March 2022 at www.apra.gov.au/sites/default/files/2022-03/Quarterly%20Private%20Health%20Insurance%20Statistics%20December%202021.pdf

ARA. (2014). Innovative funding and financing for public transport: A review of alternative, sustainable funding and financing sources. *Australasian Railway Association.* Accessed on 20 January 2017 at www.aph.gov.au/DocumentStore.ashx?id=ce430dfe-e22c-48c8-8adc-c3769f6a77de&subId=32214

Archer, R.W. (1976). The Sydney Betterment Levy, 1969–1973: an experiment in functional funding for metropolitan development. *Urban Studies,* 13, 339–342.

Asher, N. (2017). Hazelwood rehabilitation estimated to cost $743 million but may rise, Engie says. *ABC News.* 20 January 2017.

Accessed on 20 January 2017 at www.abc.net.au/news/2017-01-20/hazelwood-rehabilitation-to-cost-743-millionengie-says/8197784

Aston, H. (2015). Multinational oil and gas giants paying no petroleum resource rent tax. *Sydney Morning Herald.* 17 December 2015. Accessed on 20 January 2017 at www.smh.com.au/business/the-economy/multinational-oil-and-gas-giants-paying-no-petroleum-resource-rent-tax-20151217-glpusi.html

Auditor General. (2015). Administration of the Fifth Community Pharmacy Agreement. *Australian National Audit Office.* ANAO Report No.25 2014–15 Performance Audit. Accessed on 20 January 2017 at www.anao.gov.au/sites/g/files/net2446/f/ANAO_Report_2014-2015_25.pdf

Australian Broadcasting Corporation. (2021). Jailed former Ipswich mayor Paul Pisasale says he pleaded guilty against advice of lawyers because he 'just wanted it all over with'. *ABC News.* 16 November 2021. www.abc.net.au/news/2021-11-16/paul-pisasale-court-christopher-pinzone/100625156

Australian Bureau of Statistics. (2005). 6462.0—Information Paper: Introduction of the 15th Series Australian Consumer Price Index 2005. Accessed on 20 January 2022 at www.abs.gov.au/ausstats/abs@.nsf/Latestproducts/6462.0Media%20Release12005?opendocument&tabname=Summary&prodno=6462.0&issue=2005&num=&view=

Australian Bureau of Statistics. (2016). 8155.0—Australian Industry, 2014–15. *Australian Bureau of Statistics.* Accessed on 20 January 2017 at www.abs.gov.au/ausstats/abs@.nsf/mf/8155.0

Australian Bureau of Statistics. (2021). Australian industry. 28 May 2021. Accessed on 10 March 2022 at www.abs.gov.au/statistics/industry/industry-overview/australian-industry/latest-release

Australian Electoral Commission. (2022). Political party returns. Accessed on 10 March 2022 at transparency.aec.gov.au/AnnualPoliticalParty

REFERENCES

Australian Government. (2010). Competitive and sustainable banking system. Report by Attorney-General's Department. Accessed on 20 January 2017 at treasury.gov.au/sites/default/files/2019-03/competitive_and_sustainable_banking_system.pdf

Australian Government (2018). Australian government response to the review of pharmacy remuneration and regulation. May 2018. Accessed on 11 March 2022 at www1.health.gov.au/internet/main/publishing.nsf/content/7E5846EB2D7BA299CA257F5C007C0E21/%24File/Pharmacy-Review-Aus-Gov-Response-3-May-2018.pdf

Australian Parliament. (2020). Revenue: Budget review 2019–20 index. Accessed on 11 March 2022 at www.aph.gov.au/About_Parliament/Parliamentary_Departments/Parliamentary_Library/pubs/rp/BudgetReview201920/RevenueOverview

Australian Prudential Regulation Authority (APRA). (2021). APRA releases quarterly private health insurance statistics for March 2021. Accessed on 11 March 2022 at www.apra.gov.au/news-and-publications/apra-releases-quarterly-private-health-insurance-statistics-for-march-2021

Australian Taxation Office. (2022). Corporate tax transparency. Accessed on 11 March 2022 at data.gov.au/data/dataset/corporate-transparency

Babar, Z. and A. Vitry. (2014). Differences in Australian and New Zealand medicines funding policies. *Australian Prescriber*. NPS MedicineWise. Volume 37. Issue 5. October 2014. Accessed on 20 January 2017 at www.nps.org.au/australianprescriber/articles/differences-in-australian-and-new-zealandmedicines-funding-policies

Ballantyne, A. and S. Langcake. (2016). Why has retail inflation been so low? *Reserve Bank of Australia Bulletin*. June Quarter 2016. Accessed on 20 January 2017 at www.rba.gov.au/publications/bulletin/2016/jun/pdf/bu-0616-2.pdf

Barker, L. (2015). Who will pay the more than $17.8 billion mining rehabilitation bill? *Independent Australia*. 1 June 2015. Accessed on

20 January 2017 at independentaustralia.net/business/business-display/who-will-pay-the-178-billion-mining-rehabilitation-bill, 7772

Beck, L. and W. Jeffery. (1897). *Admiral Phillip. The Founding of New South Wales.* T. Fisher Unwin, London. Retrieved on 20 January 2017 from gutenberg.net.au/ebooks13/1302981h.html

Bentley, A. (2009). Developer sues over 'sensational' *Today Tonight* claims. *Sydney Morning Herald.* 20 October 2009. Accessed on 20 January 2017 at www.smh.com.au/business/developer-sues-over-sensational-today-tonight-claims-20091020-h6lh.html

Besser, L. (2010). Judge rejects developer's claim of defamatory report. *Age.* 19 October 2010. Accessed on 20 January 2017 at www.theage.com.au/nsw/judge-rejects-developers-claim-of-defamatory-report-20101018-16qx8.html

Boccabella, D. (2015). Using family trusts to minimise tax is on the nose: so why are policy makers silent? *The Conversation.* 22 September 2015. Accessed on 20 January 2017 at theconversation.com/using-family-trusts-to-minimise-tax-is-onthe-nose-so-why-are-policy-makers-silent-47277

Bourke, L. (2015). Bill Shorten names Cameron Milner as his new chief of staff. *Sydney Morning Herald.* 8 September 2015. Accessed on 20 January 2017 at www.smh.com.au/federal-politics/political-news/bill-shorten-names-cameron-milner-as-his-new-chief-of-staff-20150907-gjhayz.html

Britton, A. (1894). *History of New South Wales from the Records.* Edited by F.M. Bladen. Charles Potter, Government Printer, Sydney. Accessed on 20 January 2017 at aiatsis.gov.au/sites/default/files/catalogue_resources/m0045141.pdf

Brogden, J. (2015). *Submission to Productivity Commission Draft Report on Business Set-up, Transfer and Closure.* Australian Institute of Company Directors. 3 July 2015. Accessed on 20 January 2017 at www.pc.gov.au/__data/assets/pdf_file/0011/190874/subdr 043-business.pdf

Buckingham, J. (2015a). The revolving door between miners and government. Blog post. 27 March 2015. Accessed on 20 January 2017 at jeremybuckingham.org/2015/03/27/the-revolving-door-between-miners-and-government

Buckingham, J. (2015b). Revolving doors Queensland. Blog post. 27 March 2015. Accessed on 20 January 2017 at jeremybuckingham.org/2015/03/27/revolving-doors-queensland

Carty, L. and C. Trenwith. (2008). Colleagues spill beans on sex scandal town planner. *Sydney Morning Herald*. 24 February 2008. Accessed on 20 January 2017 at www.smh.com.au/articles/2008/02/23/1203 467451969.html

CBA. (2016). Annual Report 2016. *Commonwealth Bank of Australia*. Accessed on 20 January 2017 at www.commbank.com.au/content/dam/commbank/about-us/shareholders/pdfs/annualreports/2016_Annual_Report_to_Shareholders_15_August_2016.pdf

Cheng, T.C. (2013). *Does Reducing Rebates for Private Health Insurance Generate Cost Savings?*. University of Melbourne, Melbourne Institute of Applied Economic and Social Research. Accessed on 20 January 2017 at melbourneinstitute.com/downloads/policy_briefs_series/pb2013n03.pdf

Chung, D. (2008). Private provision of transport infrastructure: unveiling the inconvenient truth in New South Wales. In *Australasian Transport Research Forum* (ATRF), 31st, 2008, Gold Coast, Australia, vol. 31.

Chung, L. and S. Keoghan. (2021). Former Labor MP Craig Thomson arrested over visa fraud allegations. *Age*. 17 November 2021. Accessed on 27 April 2022. www.theage.com.au/national/nsw/former-labor-mp-craig-thomson-arrested-over-visa-fraud-allegations-20211117-p599p4.html

Clark, G. (2011). *Average Earnings and Retail Prices, UK*, 12092010. Working Paper, UC Davis.

Clarke, P. (2013). The price is wrong: pharmaceutical expenditure in Australia over the last decade and options for reform. In *Healthcare: Reform or ration*. CEDA. April 2013. Accessed on

20 January 2017 at www.ceda.com.au/ResearchAndPolicies/ Research/Health-Ageing/Healthcare-Reform-or-ration-(2013)

Collier, G. (2015). Defeated superannuation reform bid designed to fail. *Australian.* 5 December 2015. Accessed on 20 January 2017 at www.theaustralian.com.au/opinion/columnists/grace-collier/super annuationreform-implement-the-cooper-review-proposals/news-story/ a0a62c68c4d97388ae0c923d0322780a

Connolly, E. and M. Kohler. (2004). *The Impact of Superannuation on Household Saving.* Reserve Bank of Australia, Sydney.

Cooper, J. (2010). Super system review: Final report. Commonwealth of Australia. Accessed on 20 January 2017 at treasury.gov.au/review/ super-system-review

Corbett, B. (2016). Ian Macfarlane to helm Queensland Resources Council. *Australian Financial Review.* 25 September 2016. Accessed on 20 January 2017 at www.afr.com/brand/rear-window/ian-macfarlane-to-helm-queensland-resources-council-20160925-grnwvg

Crikey. (2013). Super rat spills on industry scams, gouging and dirty little secrets. *Crikey.* 9 January 2013. Accessed on 20 January 2017 at www.crikey.com.au/2013/01/09/super-rat-spills-on-industry-scams-gouging-and-dirty-little-secrets

Crikey. (2016). Smashing the revolving door. *Crikey.* 5 May 2016. Accessed on 20 January 2017 at www.crikey.com.au/2016/05/05/ crikey-says-170

Dalzell, S. and R. Hunjan. (2016). Liverpool Council chief Carl Wulff 'resigns' after asbestos contamination row, but Mayor Ned Mannoun denies he is gone. *ABC News.* 25 March 2016. Accessed on 20 January 2017 at www.abc.net.au/news/201603-16/ wulff-resigns-following-asbestos-contamination-row/7249262

Danckert, S. (2016). Future Fund, QIC and China's CIC Capital buy Port of Melbourne. *Sydney Morning Herald.* 19 September 2016. Accessed on 20 January 2017 at www.smh.com.au/business/ the-economy/future-fund-qic-and-chinas-cic-capital-buy-port-of-melbourne-20160919-grjqzx.html

Davies, A. (2015). CSG industry hires well-connected staffers. *Sydney Morning Herald*. 25 May 2015. Accessed on 20 January 2017 at www.smh.com.au/nsw/csg-industry-hires-well-connected-staffers-20150515-gh2rg3.html

Davies, A. (2018). CEO of troubled Sydney hospital resigns two days after opening. *Guardian*. 21 November 2018. Accessed on 11 March 2022 at www.theguardian.com/australia-news/2018/nov/21/ceo-of-troubled-sydney-hospital-resigns-two-days-after-opening

Deloitte. (2013). The economic and social contribution of the NSW taxi industry. *Deloitte Access Economics*. 12 December 2013. Accessed on 20 January 2017 at www2.deloitte.com/au/en/pages/economics/articles/economic-social-contribution-nsw-taxi-industry.html

Department of Education. (2022). Partnerships. *Queensland Government*. Accessed on 10 March 2022 at alt-qed.qed.qld.gov.au/programs-initiatives/department/partnerships

Devinney, T. (2013). Are university leaders really overpaid? *The Modern Cynic*. Blog. 8 May 2013. Accessed on 20 January 2017 at www.modern-cynic.org/2013/05/08/university-leaders

Donelly, B. (2015). Harper review: Pharmacists slam proposal to lift restrictions. *Sydney Morning Herald*. 1 April 2015. Accessed on 20 January 2017 at www.smh.com.au/federalpolitics/political-news/harper-review-pharmacists-slam-proposal-to-lift-restrictions-20150331-1mc84b.html

Doward, J. (2011). Glencore denies allegations over copper mine tax. *Guardian*. Accessed on 14 March 2022 at www.theguardian.com/business/2011/apr/17/glencore-denies-copper-tax-allegations

Drolia, R. (2016). Vedanta Ltd wins first ever auction of an Indian gold mine. *Times of India*. 27 February 2016. Accessed on 20 January 2017 at timesofindia.indiatimes.com/business/india-business/Vedanta-Ltd-wins-first-ever-auction-of-an-Indian-gold-mine/articleshow/51165549.cms

Drolia, R. (2017). Chhattisgarh auctions India's most expensive limestone block. *Times of India*. 2 May 2017. Accessed on 10 March 2022 at timesofindia.indiatimes.com/city/raipur/chhattisgarh-auctions-indias-most-expensive-limestone-block/articleshow/58478468.cms

Duckett, S. (2013a). *Australia's Bad Drug Deal: High pharmaceutical prices*. Grattan Institute. Accessed on 20 January 2017 at grattan. edu.au/wp-content/uploads/2014/04/Australias_Bad_Drug_Deal_FINAL.pdf

Duckett, S. (2013b). Public–private hospital partnerships are risky business. *The Conversation*. 30 July 2013. Accessed on 20 January 2017 at theconversation.com/public-private-hospital-partnerships-are-risky-business-16421

Duckett, S. (2017). *Cutting a Better Drug Deal*. Grattan Institute. Accessed on 11 March 2022 at grattan.edu.au/wp-content/uploads/2017/03/886-Cutting-a-better-drug-deal.pdf

Duckett, S. and K. Nemet. (2019). *The History and Purposes of Private Health Insurance*. Grattan Institute. Accessed on 11 March 2022 at grattan.edu.au/wp-content/uploads/2019/07/190715-WP-The-history-and-purposes-of-private-health-insurance-ISBN-Updated.pdf

Dunlevy, G. (2009a). Rowe quit weeks before corruption storm: Bligh. *Brisbane Times*. 31 July 2009. Accessed on 20 January 2017 at www.brisbanetimes.com.au/queensland/rowe-quit-weeks-before-corruption-storm-bligh-20090731-e4a7.html

Dunlevy, G. (2009b). QIC chairman Trevor Rowe to step down. *Sydney Morning Herald*. 31 July 2009. Accessed on 20 January 2017 at www.smh.com.au/business/qic-chairman-trevor-rowe-to-step-down-20090730-e39b.html

Elaurant, S. and W. McDougall. (2014). Politics, funding and transport: the need for systematic reform. In Australian Institute of Traffic Planning and Management National Conference, 2014, Adelaide, South Australia, Australia (No. 2).

Electoral Commission Queensland. (2022). Donor location map. Accessed on 10 March 2022 at disclosures.ecq.qld.gov.au/Map?resetNav=true

Environmental Justice Australia. (2016). *Dodging clean up costs: Six tricks coal mining companies play*. Report. Accessed on 20 January 2017 at envirojustice.org.au/sites/default/files/files/EJA_Dodging_clean_up_costs.pdf

REFERENCES

Etheridge, D. (2012). Director interlocking in Australia. PhD Thesis. University of Western Australia.

Evans, J. (2021). Police find no evidence of criminal conduct in $33 million Leppington Triangle airport land purchase. *ABC News*. 29 September 2021. Accessed on 27 April 2022 at www.abc.net. au/news/2021-09-29/leppington-triangle-airport-land-purchase-no-criminal-conduct/100500294

Farrell, P. and O. Laughland. (2014). Tony Abbott's daughter was courted for scholarship. *Guardian*. 22 May 2014. Accessed on 20 January 2017 at www.theguardian.com/world/2014/may/22/frances-abbott-courted-scholarship-new-matilda

Fernyhough, J. (2020). CBA to divest majority of Aussie in Lendi merger. *Australian Financial Review*. 16 December 2020. Accessed on 10 March 2022 at www.afr.com/companies/financial-services/cba-to-divest-majority-of-aussie-in-lendi-merger-20201216-p56nzg

Fletcher, P. (2013). Superannuation's Role in Advancing the Power and Economic Influence of the Union Movement. Speech to HR Nicholls Society, 6 August 2013. Accessed on 10 March 2022 at www.paul fletcher.com.au/other-speeches/superannuations-role-in-advancing-the-power-and-economic-influence-of-the-union

Foster, G., P. Frijters and A. Ko. (2018). A tale of cyclones, exports, and surplus foregone in Australia's protected banana industry. *Economic Record*, vol. 94, no. 306, pp. 276–300

Frank, T. (2016). Forget the FBI cache; the Podesta emails show how America is run. *Guardian*. 31 October 2016. Accessed on 20 January 2017 at www.theguardian.com/commentisfree/2016/oct/31/the-podesta-emails-show-who-runs-america-and-how-they-do-it

Frijters, P. (2013). Timothy Devinney on overpaid vice chancellors. *Core Economics*. Blog. 15 May 2013. Accessed on 20 January 2017 at economics.com.au/2013/05/15/timothy-devinney-on-overpaid-vice-chancellors

Frijters, P. (2016). Could sortition help against corruption, Part II. *Club Troppo*. Blogpost. 19 September 2016. Accessed on 20 January

2017 at clubtroppo.com.au/2016/09/19/could-sortition-help-against-corruption-part-ii

Frijters, P. (2021). Citizen-jury appointments? *Club Troppo*. Blogpost. 24 June 2021. Accessed on 11 March 2022 at clubtroppo.com.au/2021/06/24/citizen-jury-appointments

Frijters, P., G. Foster and M. Baker. (2021). *The Great Covid Panic: What Happened, Why, and What To Do Next*. The Brownstone Institute.

Gambetta, D. (2009). *Codes of the underworld: How criminals communicate*. Princeton University Press, Princeton, NJ.

Gittins, R. (2015). We're letting superannuation providers rip us off. *Sydney Morning Herald*. 28 April 2015. Accessed on 20 January 2017 at www.smh.com.au/comment/were-letting-superannuation-providers-rip-us-off-20150428-1muw57.html

Grudnoff, M. (2013). *Pouring More Fuel on the Fire: The nature and extent of federal government subsidies to the mining industry*. The Australia Institute. Policy Brief No. 52. June 2013. Accessed on 20 January 2016 at australiainstitute.org.au/wp-content/uploads/2020/12/PB-52-Pouring-more-fuel-on-the-fire.pdf

Grudnoff, M. (2015). *A Super Waste of Money: Redesigning super tax concessions*. The Australia Institute. April 2015. Accessed on 20 January 2017 at australiainstitute.org.au/report/a-super-waste-of-money-redesigning-super-tax-concessions/

Gruen, N. (2014). Central banking for the people: A modest proposal for radical change. Accessed on 20 January 2017 at www.nesta.org.uk/report/central-banking-for-all-a-modest-case-for-radical-reform/

Hall, D. (2014). *Why public–private Partnerships don't work: The many advantages of the public alternative*. Public Services International Research Unit, University of Greenwich. January 2014. Accessed on 11 May 2022 at www.world-psi.org/sites/default/files/rapport_eng_56pages_a4_lr.pdf

Han, M. (2016). Thomas Piketty debunks Australia's meritocracy 'fairy tale'. *Australia Financial Review*. 23 October 2016. Accessed on

14 March 2022 at www.afr.com/news/economy/thomas-piketty-debunks-australias-meritocracy-fairy-tale-20161023-gs8sb6

Hannam, P. (2021). Train in vain: how NSW's new public transport body led to a budget standoff. *The Guardian*. 15 December 2021. Accessed on 9 March 2022 at www.theguardian.com/australia-news/2021/dec/15/train-in-vain-how-nsws-new-public-transport-body-led-to-a-budget-standoff

Harper, I., P. Anderson, S. McCluskey and M. O'Brien. (2015). *Competition Policy Review Final Report*. Australian Government Treasury. Accessed on 20 January 2017 at competitionpolicyreview.gov.au/files/2015/03/Competition-policy-review-report_online.pdf

Harvey, K. (2011a). Pharmacies to push supplements as 'fries and Coke' to prescriptions. *The Conversation*. 27 September 2011. Accessed on 20 January 2017 at theconversation.com/pharmacies-to-push-supplements-as-fries-and-coke-to-prescriptions-3578

Harvey, K. (2011b). One wrong foot after another: the ethics of the Pharmacy Guild's deals. *The Conversation*. 20 October 2011. Accessed on 20 January 2017 at theconversation.com/one-wrong-foot-after-another-the-ethics-of-the-pharmacy-guilds-deals-3939

Hawthorne, M. (2009). Why BrisConnections has courted battle with unit holders. *Sydney Morning Herald*. 28 March 2009. Accessed on 20 January 2017 at www.smh.com.au/business/why-brisconnections-has-courted-battle-with-unit-holders-20090327-9eca.html

Hewett, J. (2016). Coalition's super changes hurt rather than help. *Australian Financial Review*. 23 November 2016. Accessed on 20 January 2017 at www.afr.com/opinion/columnists/super-changes-dont-add-up-long-term-20161123-gsvyh3v

Huey Yeoh, Y. (2021). Superannuation Funds Management Services in Australia. Australia Industry (ANZIC) Report K6419D Financial and Insurance Services. June 2021. IBISWorld.

Iggulden, T. (2019). Christopher Pyne called out for taking defence job within 18 months of leaving parliament. *ABC News*. 27 June 2019. Accessed on 10 March 2022 at www.abc.net.au/news/2019-06-27/christopher-pyne-called-out-for-taking-defence-job/11250526

Industry Commission. (1991). *Mining and Minerals Processing in Australia. Vol. 3: Issues in Details.* Report Number 7. 25 February 1991. Accessed on 20 January 2017 at www.pc.gov.au/inquiries/completed/mining/07miningv3.pdf

Ison, R. (2015). MP alleges misconduct in councils. *Courier Mail.* 14 October 2015. Accessed on 20 January 2017 at www.couriermail.com.au/news/queensland/queenslandgovernment/mp-alleges-misconduct-in-councils/news-story/d446fde1853936de862cdf8ac490debc

Jacks, T. (2015). Private schools benefit from more than $2 billion in government funding. *Age.* 30 December 2015. Accessed on 20 January 2017 at www.theage.com.au/victoria/private-schools-benefit-from-more-than-2-billion-in-government-funding-20151230-glwups.html

Keane, B. (2021). A Murdoch consigliere to run the ACCC? How very Australian—and very wrong. *Crikey.* 16 December 2021. Accessed on 10 March 2022 at www.crikey.com.au/2021/12/16/murdoch-mate-run-accc-very-australian-very-wrong

Keen, L. (2016). Former ANZ CEO Mike Smith takes PwC 'ambassadorial role' to expand Asia practice. *Australian Financial Review.* 13 September 2016. Accessed on 20 January 2017 at www.afr.com/business/accounting/former-anz-ceo-mike-smith-takes-pwc-ambassadorial-role-to-expand-asia-practice-20160912-greezq

Khadem, N. (2019). ATO says multinationals disputing billions in tax bills amid crackdown on profit shifting. *ABC News.* 24 December 2019. Accessed on 11 March 2022 at www.abc.net.au/news/2019-12-24/multinationals-dispute-ato-tax-bills/11823074

Kidd, R. and T. Thompson. (2013). UQ senior staff turned blind eye to 'dodgy deal' to get vice-chancellor Paul Greenfield's daughter into school of medicine. *Courier-Mail.* 14 September 2013. Accessed on 27 April 2022 at www.couriermail.com.au/news/queensland/uq-senior-staff-turned-blind-eye-to-8216dodgy-deal8217-to-get-vice-chancellor-paul-greenfield8217s-daughter-into-school-of-medicine/news-story/12c650dc03cdf0aa6b2051e35834581d

King, S. (2013). Groceries, power and fuel: crunch time for competition review. *The Conversation.* 17 December 2013. Accessed on 20 January 2017 at theconversation.com/groceries-power-and-fuel-crunch-time-for-competition-review-21403

Knott, M. (2011). The power index: Australia's most powerful lobbyist is . . . Kos Sclavos. *Crikey.* 2 December 2011. Accessed on 20 January 2017 at www.crikey.com.au/2011/12/02/the-power-index-australias-most-powerful-lobbyist-is-kos-sclavos

Kuyper, J.W. and F. Wolkenstein. (2019). Complementing and correcting representative institutions: When and how to use mini-publics. *European Journal of Political Research*, vol. 58, no. 2, pp. 656–675.

Leigh, A. (2013). *Battlers and Billionaires: The story of inequality in Australia.* Black Inc., Melbourne.

Letts, S. (2016). Banks facing $180 million compensation payments for gouging fees without advice. *ABC News.* 26 October 2016. Accessed on 20 January 2017 at www.abc.net.au/news/2016-10-27/banks-facing-180-million-compensation-payments/7971006

Liu, K. and B.R. Arnold. (2012). *Superannuation and Insurance: Related parties and member cost.* Working Paper. November 2012. Australian Prudential Regulation Authority. Accessed on 20 January 2017 at www.apra.gov.au/AboutAPRA/Documents/SA_WP_SIRPMC_102012_ex.pdf

Loader, C. (2016). Traffic volumes on Australian toll roads. *Charting Transport: Looking at transport through graphs and maps.* Blog post. Accessed on 20 January 2017 at chartingtransport.com/2012/03/03/traffic-volumes-on-australian-toll-roads

Long, S. (2016). Corporate tax minimisation costs governments $US1 trillion says accounting insider. *ABC News.* Accessed on 20 January 2017 at www.abc.net.au/news/2016-07-11/corporate-tax-minimisation-costs-governments-1-trillion/7587092

Lynham, A. (2016). Explorer concession supports Qld resource sector. Media statement. 17 February 2016. Accessed on 20 January 2017 at statements.qld.gov.au/Statement/2016/2/17/explorerconcession-supports-qld-resource-sector

Mannix, L. (2015). Revolving regulators: How one door opens another in Australia's financial system. *Sydney Morning Herald*. 25 July 2015. Accessed on 20 January 2017 at www.smh.com.au/business/revolving-regulators-how-one-door-opens-another-in-australias-financial-system-20150527-ghb6n4

Marlton, A. (2016). Can anyone remember the last time they saw the fair go? Maybe we just imagined it? *Guardian*. 28 October 2016. Accessed on 20 January 2017 at www.theguardian.com/commentisfree/2016/oct/28/can-anyone-remember-the-last-time-they-saw-the-fair-go-maybe-we-just-imagined-it?CMP=Share_iOSApp_Other

Martin, R.E. and R.C. Hill. (2012). Measuring Baumol and Bowen Effects in Public Research Universities. Working paper. Available at SSRN. Accessed on 14 March 2022 at papers.ssrn.com/sol3/papers.cfm?abstract_id=2153122

Mastrobuoni, G. (2015). The value of connections: evidence from the Italian-American Mafia. *Economic Journal*, vol. 125, no. 586, F256–F288.

Mathieson, C. (2009). Unravelling Rowe's tangled web. *Australian*. 10 August 2009. Accessed on 20 January 2017 at www.theaustralian.com.au/business/latest/unravelling-rowes-tangled-web/news-story/5ef63a8b6d543d273c54a295758e3c82?nk=2b2106e4b89909f27f2065b46302b178-1472445336

McCarthy, J. (2013). State's top public servants are jumping ship to join the CSG industry they assessed. *Courier Mail*. 1 April 2013. Accessed on 20 January 2017 at www.couriermail.com.au/business/states-top-public-servants-are-jumping-ship-to-join-the-csg-industry-they-assessed/newsstory/802ca4515b47841a8b516babd2cdd6f1?sv=a79738c6c40614be49a0ae9e5f8c6375&nk=2b2106e4b89909f27f2065b4 6302b178-1484985297

McClymont, K. (2015). Former union boss Michael Williamson can't explain the missing millions. *Sydney Morning Herald*. Accessed on 14 March 2022 at www.smh.com.au/nsw/former-union-boss-michael-williamson-cant-explain-the-missing-millions-20150410-1migrn.html

REFERENCES

McCreadie, K. (2012). *Stop Not Till the Goal Is Reached: The 10 principles for fearless success that inspired Maha Sinnathamby to build a city.* Wiley, Brisbane.

McCutcheon, P. (2017). Adani bought India flights for Queensland mayors of councils paying $30m for company airstrip. *ABC News.* 30 October 2017. Accessed on 10 March 2022 at www.abc.net.au/news/2017-10-30/adani-bought-india-flights-queensland-mayors-funding-airstrip/9100332?sf128469273=1

McKenna, M. (2012). Campbell Newman's father-in-law Frank Monsour breaks silence. *Australian.* 2 February 2012. Accessed on 20 January 2017 at www.theaustralian.com.au/national-affairs/campbell-newmans-father-in-law-frank-monsour-breaks-silence/news-story/f66d87c9ca60aa3ec4854328779add0a?nk=2b2106e4b-89909f27f2065b4630 2b178-1485733816

Menadue, J. (2015). Democratic renewal; vested interests and the subversion of the public interest? *Pearls and Irritations: John Menadue's public policy journal.* Blog. 13 May 2015. Accessed on 20 January 2017 at johnmenadue.com/blog/?p=3758

Menadue, J. and M. Keating (eds). (2015). *Fairness, Opportunity and Security: Filling the policy vacuum.* ATF Press, Adelaide.

Minifie, J. (2016). PC sets groundwork for long-awaited look at super competition and efficiency. *The Conversation.* 3 August 2016. Accessed on 20 January 2017 at theconversation.com/pc-sets-groundwork-for-long-awaited-look-at-super-competition-and-efficiency-63395

Ministry of Petroleum and Energy. (2017). The Petroleum Tax System. Norwegian Petroleum Directorate. Accessed on 20 January 2017 at www.norskpetroleum.no/en/economy/petroleum-tax

Mitchell, S. (2013). Mexican standoff: Woolworths takes aim at Aldi over packaging. *Sydney Morning Herald.* 10 December 2013. Accessed on 20 January 2017 at www.smh.com.au/business/retail/mexican-standoff-woolworths-takes-aim-at-aldi-over-packaging-20131209-2z2cv

Murray, C.K. (2014). Uber's $16 billion flag fall. *MacroBusiness*. Accessed on 20 January 2017 at www.macrobusiness.com.au/2014/06/ubers-6billion-threat-to-taxi-licence-owners

Murray, C.K. (2016a) At the first interval: evaluating ACT's Land Value Tax Transition. Prosper Australia. Accessed on 20 January 2017 at www.prosper.org.au/wp-content/uploads/2016/09/The-First-interval-Evaluating-ACTs-Land-Valur-Tax-Transition.pdf

Murray, Cameron K. (2016b). When Reciprocity Becomes Back-Scratching: An economic inquiry PhD Thesis, School of Economics, The University of Queensland. doi:10.14264/ uql.2016.88

Murray, C.K. and P. Frijters (2016). Clean money, dirty system: Connected landowners capture beneficial land rezoning. *Journal of Urban Economics*, vol. 93, pp. 99–114.

Murray, C.K., P. Frijters and M. Vorster. (2015). *Give and You Shall Receive: The Emergence of Welfare-Reducing Reciprocity*. IZA Discussion Paper No. 9010.

Murray, C.K., P. Frijters and M. Vorster. (2017). The back-scratching game. *Journal of Economic Behavior and Organization*, vol. 142, pp. 494–508.

New South Wales Parliament. (2020). *Operation and Management of the Northern Beaches Hospital*. Accessed on 11 March 2022 at www.parliament.nsw.gov.au/lcdocs/inquiries/2524/Final%20Report%20No.%2052%20-%20Operation%20and%20management%20of%20the%20Northern%20Beaches%20Hospital.pdf

Odgers, J. (2002). An initial performance review of Melbourne's City Link [sic] toll road. 25th Australian Transport Research Forum. Canberra.

OECD. (2011). Pension funds at a glance: Pension fund operating costs and fees. *OECD iLibrary*. 17 March 2011. Accessed on 20 January 2017 at www.oecd-ilibrary.org/finance-and-investment/pensions-at-a-glance-2011/pension-fund-operating-costs-and-fees_pension_glance-2011-43-en;jsessionid=93813p3eejj5s.xoecd-live-03

OECD. (2017). Funded pension indicators. *OECD.Stat*. Accessed on 14 March 2022 at stats.oecd.org/viewhtml.aspx?QueryName=14477&QueryType=View

Olson, M. (1965). *The Logic of Collective Action: Public goods and the theory of groups.* Harvard University Press, Cambridge, MA.

Olson, M. (1982). *The Rise and Decline of Nations: Economic growth, stagnation, and social rigidities.* Yale University Press, New Haven, CT.

Overington, C. (2016). Mind over body. Australian. 24–25 September 2016. Accessed on 20 January 2017 at www.theaustralian.com. au/life/weekend-australian-magazine/mind-over-body/news-story/ 12f2e59aacd99113011bf3c30f441f5e?nk=2b2106e4b89909f27f206 5b46302b178-1474846729

Patrick, A. (2016). Inside story: How ANZ paid Mike Smith $88m for failed Asian strategy. *Australian Financial Review.* 28 July 2016. Accessed on 20 January 2017 at www.afr.com/business/ banking-and-finance/inside-story-how-anz-paid-mike-smith-88m- for-failed-asian-strategy-20160610-gpgbp3

Patty, A. (2016). Fee rise for new property owners ahead of land titles office privatisation. *Sydney Morning Herald.* 6 June 2016. Accessed on 20 January 2017 at www.smh.com.au/business/the- economy/fee-rise-for-new-property-owners-ahead-of-land-titles- office-privatisation-20160605-gpbwxp.html

Peel, M., R. Campbell and R. Denniss. (2014). *Mining the Age of Entitlement: State government assistance to the minerals and fossil fuel sector.* The Australia Institute. Technical Brief No. 31, June 2014. Accessed on 20 January 2017 at australiainstitute.org.au/ report/mining-the-age-of-entitlement/

Potter, B. (2016). Ex-ACCI chief slams monopolists and exploiters. *Australian Financial Review.* 4 August 2016. Accessed on 20 January 2017 at www.afr.com/news/ex-acci-chief-slams-monopolists-and- exploiters-20160804-gql7cw

Productivity Commission. (2005). *Economic Implications of an Ageing Australia.* Productivity Commission Research Report.

Productivity Commission. (2006). *Economic Impacts of Migration and Population Growth.* Productivity Commission Research Report, 24 April 2006. Accessed on 20 January 2017 at www.pc.gov.au/

inquiries/completed/migration-population/report/migrationand population.pdf

Productivity Commission. (2009). *Government Drought Support.* Productivity Commission Inquiry Report, No. 46, 27 February 2009. Accessed on 20 January 2017 at www.pc.gov.au/inquiries/completed/drought/report/drought-support.pdf

Productivity Commission. (2011). *Economic Regulation of Airport Services.* Productivity Commission Inquiry Report, No. 57, 14 December 2011. Accessed on 20 January 2017 at www.pc.gov.au/inquiries/completed/airport-regulation/report/airport-regulation.pdf

Productivity Commission. (2015). PC productivity update 2015. Accessed on 14 March 2022 at www.pc.gov.au/research/ongoing/productivity-update/pc-productivity-update-2015

Productivity Commission. (2019). Superannuation: assessing efficiency and competitiveness. Productivity Commission Inquiry Report, No. 91, 21 December 2018. Accessed on 10 March 2022 at www.pc.gov.au/inquiries/completed/superannuation/assessment/report/superannuation-assessment.pdf

Pruaitch, P. (2016). 2017 National Budget. Independent State of Papua New Guinea. Accessed on 20 January 2017 at www.treasury.gov.pg/html/national_budget/files/2017/2017%20Treasurer's%20Budget%20Speech.pdf

Rice Warner. (2014). Superannuation Fees. Submission to Financial System Inquiry. July 2014. Accessed on 20 January 2017 at www.ricewarner.com/superannuation-fees-financial-system-inquiry/

Richardson, D. (2018). Abolish the cashing out of franking credits: Inquiry into the Implications of Removing Refundable Franking Credits: submission. The Australia Institute. November 2018. Accessed on 11 March 2022 at australiainstitute.org.au/wp-content/uploads/2020/12/Cashing-out-franking-credits-WEB.pdf

Richardson, D. and R. Denniss. (2011). *Mining the truth: The rhetoric and reality of the commodities boom.* The Australia Institute. Institute Paper No. 7, September 2011. Accessed on 20 January 2017 at australiainstitute.org.au/wp-content/uploads/2020/12/Mining-the-truth-IP7_4.pdf

Riga, R. (2019). Ipswich City Council former CEO sentenced to five years in jail for corruption. *ABC News*. 15 February 2019. Accessed on 11 May 2022 at www.abc.net.au/news/2019-02-15/ipswich-city-council-ceo-carl-wulff-sentenced-for-corruption/10814924

Robertson, J. (2016). Jackie Trad launched 'expletive-ridden attack', says MP Rob Pyne. *Guardian*. 19 April 2016. Accessed on 20 January 2017 at www.theguardian.com/australia-news/2016/apr/19/jackie-trad-launched-expletive-ridden-attack-says-mp-rob-pyne

Robin, M. (2015). 'A proposal to gut journalism in Australia': corporate directors want less transparency. *Crikey*. 9 July 2015. Accessed on 20 January 2017 at www.crikey.com.au/2015/07/09/a-proposal-to-gut-journalism-in-australia-corporate-directors-want-less-transparency

Rosen, S. (2010). *Australia's Oldest House: Surgeon John Harris and Experiment Farm Cottage*. Halstead Press, Sydney.

Rowlands, J. and R. Boden. (2020). How Australian vice-chancellors' pay came to average $1 million and why it's a problem. *The Conversation*. 2 December 2020. Accessed on 11 March 2022 at theconversation.com/how-australian-vice-chancellors-pay-came-to-average-1-million-and-why-its-a-problem-150829

Ryan, P. (2016). FIRB boss shelves controversial plans to take advisory role at private equity company. *ABC News*. 5 October 2016. Accessed on 27 April 2022 at www.abc.net.au/news/2016-10-05/firb-boss-shelves-controversial-plans-to-take-advisory-role/7906248

Sandroni, P. (2010). A new financial instrument of value capture in São Paulo: certificates of additional construction potential. In G. Ingram and Y. Hong (eds). *Municipal Revenues and Land Policies*. Lincoln Institute of Land Policy, Cambridge, MA. Accessed on 14 March 2022 at *Blog: Paulo Sandroni*, sandroni.com.br/?page_id=310

Schneiders, B. and R. Millar (2016). CityLink users to be slugged tens of billions under Andrews government plan. *Sydney Morning Herald*.

5 February 2016. Accessed on 20 January 2017 at www.smh.com. au/business/citylink-users-to-be-slugged-tens-of-billions-under-andrews-government-plan-20160204-gmmahg.html

Schwab, A. (2010). *Pigs at the Trough: Lessons from Australia's decade of corporate greed.* Wiley, Brisbane.

Seccombe, M. (2016). Who foots the bill for open-cut mine rehabilitation? *The Saturday Paper.* February 2016. Accessed on 20 January 2017 at www.thesaturdaypaper.com.au/news/politics/2016/02/06/who-foots-the-bill-open-cut-mine-rehabilitation/14546772002857

Services Australia (2021). Annual report 2020–21. Accessed on 10 March 2022 at www.servicesaustralia.gov.au/sites/default/files/annual-report-2020-21.pdf

Sims, R. (2016). Keynote Address. RBB Economics Conference. *ACCC: Australian Competition & Consumer Commission.* 26 October 2016. Accessed on 20 January 2017 at www.accc.gov.au/speech/keynote-address-rbb-economics-conference-0

Skulley, M. (2013). CFMEU stirs up anti-Cbus campaign over Grocon. *Australian Financial Review.* 7 January 2013. Accessed on 20 January 2017 at http://www.afr.com/business/construction/cfmeu-stirs-up-anticbus-campaign-over-grocon-20130106-je9u1

Smith, T. (2020). University vice-chancellor salaries are 'ridiculous'. *Macquarie University.* 16 November 2020. Accessed on 11 March 2022 at researchers.mq.edu.au/en/clippings/university-vice-chancellor-salaries-are-ridiculous

Solomons, M. and M. Willacy. (2014). QCoal's James Mackay developing environmental policy for Newman Government in Queensland. *ABC News.* 5 May 2014. Accessed on 20 January 2017 at www.abc.net.au/news/2014-05-05/qcoals-james-mackay-developing-environmental-policy-for-lnp/5431008

Spence, E. (2013). The 'perfect injustice': is Australia more corrupt than we think? *The Conversation.* 14 February 2013. Accessed on 20 January 2017 at theconversation.com/the-perfect-injustice-is-australia-more-corrupt-than-we-think-12108

REFERENCES

Standen, C. (2018). Privatising WestConnex is the biggest waste of public funds for corporate gain in Australian history. *The Conversation*. 25 September 2018. Accessed on 9 March 2022 at theconversation.com/privatising-westconnex-is-the-biggest-waste-of-public-funds-for-corporate-gain-in-australian-history-102790

Thomsen, S. (2017). Bill Shorten plans to tax family trusts at the same level as companies. *Business Insider Australia*. 31 July 2017. Accessed on 11 March 2022 at www.businessinsider.com.au/bill-shorten-plans-to-tax-family-trusts-at-the-same-level-as-companies-2017-7

Tlozek, E. (2013). Ipswich City Council chief executive Carl Wulff quits amid misconduct investigation. *ABC News*. 13 December 2013. Accessed on 10 March 2022 at www.abc.net.au/news/2013-12-13/ipswich-council-chief-executive-quits-amid-cmc-investigation/5156234

Treasury. (2013). *A Super Charter: Fewer changes, better outcomes*. A report to the Treasurer and Minister Assisting for Financial Services and Superannuation. Accessed on 20 January 2017 at treasury.gov.au/sites/default/files/2019-03/super_charter_report.pdf

Treasury. (2016). Tax Expenditures Statement 2015. Commonwealth of Australia. Accessed on 20 January 2017 at treasury.gov.au/publication/tax-expenditures-statement-2015

Treasury. (2020). *Statement 5: Revenue*. Budget Paper No. 1. Accessed on 10 March 2022 at budget.gov.au/2021-22/content/bp1/download/bp1_bs5.pdf

Treasury. (2021). *2021 Intergenerational report: Australia over the next 40 years*. Accessed on 10 March 2022 at treasury.gov.au/sites/default/files/2021-06/p2021-182464.pdf

Turchin, P. (2007). *War and Peace and War: The rise and fall of empires*. Penguin, New York, NY.

Tyson, J. (2014). *Reforming Tax Expenditures in Italy: What, why, and how?* IMF Working Paper WP/14/7. International Monetary Fund. Accessed on 20 January 2017 at www.imf.org/external/pubs/ft/wp/2014/wp1407.pdf

Uhlmann, C., A. Greene and S. Anderson. (2016). Chinese donors to Australian political parties: who gave how much? *ABC News*. 21 August 2016. Accessed on 20 January 2017 at www.abc.net.au/news/2016-08-21/china-australia-political-donations/7766654

Vidot, A. and L. Barbour. (2014). Dry argument: Australia's drought policy dilemma. *ABC News*. 24 February 2014. Accessed on 14 March 2022 at www.abc.net.au/news/2014-02-21/drought-assistance-in-australia/5269062

Wade, M. (2005). Libs favour rich as Labor picks the rest. *Sydney Morning Herald*. 14 May 2005. Accessed on 20 January 2017 at www.smh.com.au/news/National/Libs-favour-rich-as-Labor-picks-the-rest/2005/05/13/1115843374425.html

Wakatama, G. (2014). Disgraced Eddie Obeid stripped of Order of Australia medal in wake of ICAC corruption findings. *ABC News*. 17 December 2014. Accessed on 20 January 2017 at www.abc.net.au/news/2014-12-16/eddie-obeid-stripped-of-order-of-australia-medal/5970690

Walsh, L. (2020). Prostitutes and bags full of cash: the downfall of a local mayor. *Australian Financial Review*. 17 October 2020. Accessed on 10 March 2022 at www.afr.com/politics/prostitutes-and-bags-full-of-cash-the-downfall-of-a-local-mayor-20201015-p565fa

West, M. (2014). Glencore tax bill on $15b income: Zip, zilch, zero. *Sydney Morning Herald*. 27 June 2014. Accessed on 20 January 2017 at www.smh.com.au/business/glencore-tax-bill-on-15b-income-zip-zilch-zero-20140626-3awg0.html

West, M. (2016). Sheepish stewards of ASIC sale face a sceptical Senate. *MichaelWestMedia*. 2 October 2016. Accessed on 20 January 2017 at www.michaelwest.com.au/sheepish-stewards-of-asic-sale-face-sceptical-senate

West, M. (2021). Revealed: Australia's top 40 tax dodgers for 2021. *MichaelWestMedia*. 15 January 2021. Accessed on 11 March 2022 at www.michaelwest.com.au/revealed-australias-top-40-tax-dodgers-for-2021

REFERENCES

Witsenhuysen, F. (2016). New CEO of LVRC ready for big role. *Gatton, Lockyer & Brisbane Valley Star*. 10 August 2016. Accessed on 20 January 2017 at www.couriermail.com.au/news/queensland/gatton/new-ceo-of-lvrc-ready-for-big-role/news-story/d0c898b65a3b2d8db3632e9cd846b3ca

Wright, S. and E. Bagshaw (2019). The cost of drought—and it's just going to grow. *Sydney Morning Herald*. 3 November 2019. Accessed on 11 March 2022 at www.smh.com.au/politics/federal/the-cost-of-drought-and-it-s-just-going-to-grow-20191102-p536rd.html

Yates, C. (2016). CBA shareholders in the money 25 years after the float. *Sydney Morning Herald*. 13 September 2016. Accessed on 20 January 2017 at www.smh.com.au/business/banking-and-finance/cba-shareholders-in-the-money-25-years-after-float-20160912-gre7i9.html

Notes

1   According to World Bank data, Australia overtook comparable nations such as Canada and the UK in the Gini index, a measure of income inequality, between 2008 and 2010. Andrew Leigh in his 2013 book *Battlers and Billionaires* assembled much of the available statistics on inequality and concluded that inequality was lowest in the 1970s. On a recent visit to Australia, French economist Thomas Piketty made the point that 'the high after-tax rate of return on wealth, combined with low rates of economic growth, means wealth inequality in the 21st century may reach or even surpass the 19th century "oligarchic" levels' (Han, 2016).

2   Thanks to drought, and perhaps his involvement with organised gambling that led to him being charged in 1797, though never convicted, James Ruse died with little land and few possessions. The first James to play the Game of Mates in Australia came to a dismal end.

3   We are referring to a 2016 incident involving a journalist reporting some of our research.

4   See Archer (1976) for a detailed analysis of this levy. A report by the Australasian Railway Association to the New South Wales parliament in 2013 discusses this betterment levy and other historical ones that were used to fund investment in public works such as rail, water and sewer infrastructure (ARA, 2014).

5   Property developers seem very keen to claim defamation following media coverage of their activities. For example, Gold Coast property developer Craig Gore sued his former business associate, Sydney builder Ivan McFadyen, as well as his former helicopter pilot and the pilot's wife, over comments made on the current affairs television show *Today Tonight* that exposed his dodgy business dealings (Bentley, 2009). Sydney property developer Antoine Bechara lost a

court case claiming he was defamed in confidential police complaints (Besser, 2010). There are many more such examples.

6 You wouldn't believe it, but the contractor who built Australia's first toll road was also a James—James Harrex. He arrived a convict, was emancipated, built many of the first roads out of Sydney, but was later convicted of cattle theft. Once a James, always a James.

7 Refer to Appendix: Economic Loss from Transport PPP Projects for the calculation method.

8 The loss is probably higher still because we are not here calculating the additional fees and tolls that James was able to get via the various hidden clauses in the PPP contracts.

9 A chilling account of the multiple scams that fuel the superannuation industry by an anonymous insider can be found in Crikey (2013).

10 This also implies that by just this effect alone, the whole compulsory superannuation scheme is one-third less effective at promoting personal savings behaviour than intended.

11 This total is the product of $19.4 billion, which comes from concessional taxation of income being diverted to superannuation funds, and the rest from reduced taxation on earnings from super funds themselves (Treasury, 2020). Of course, because of changes in behaviour, removing these concessions will not generate all of the potential revenue.

12 You can find an analysis of these hidden costs and fees in a 2014 report by financial consultants Rice Warner (Rice Warner, 2014) submitted to the federal government's Financial System Inquiry. The Organisation for Economic Co-operation and Development (OECD) also makes available international comparisons of superannuation overhead costs (OECD, 2017).

13 Compulsory superannuation is one of the drivers of the relatively high growth of the financial services industry. So large has the cost of finance become in the economy that the 2005 change to the Consumer Price Index added a category for financial services to include fees and charges for banking, loans and for insurance, on which they estimated the average household was spending 9% of their income (Australian Bureau of Statistics, 2005).

14 The inquiry by the Productivity Commission on how to assess the competitiveness and efficiency of the superannuation industry is the latest in a long line of technical reviews and consultation processes looking to lay the groundwork for radical change of the system: see commentary on this review in Minifie (2016).

15 The review was chaired by Jeremy Cooper, hence the common name. However, the review was actually called the 'Review into the Governance, Efficiency, Structure and Operation of Australia's Superannuation System'. It released its final report in July 2010 (Cooper, 2010).

16 Such as a bizarre column in the *Australian Financial Review* by Jennifer Hewett who attempts to scare the reader by claiming this tiny change will force people onto the old-age pension (Hewett, 2016).

17 Such as Gordon Nuttall, a former Queensland minister who was gaoled for corruptly receiving payments, and Eddie Obeid, former New South Wales Labor party MP, who was gaoled in 2016 for giving grey gifts to businesses he had a joint interest in with his extended family.

18 For example, former prime minister Tony Abbott's daughter was given a 'chairman's scholarship' worth $60,000 by an organisation whose chairman was a Liberal party donor and personal friend of Tony Abbott (Farrell and Laughland, 2014).

19 South Australian Lobbyist Register, entry for GC Advisory Pty Ltd. n.d. Accessed on 10 March 2022 at https://www.lobbyists.sa.gov.au/#/lobbyist/121

20 We conducted these experiments on over 400 students at the University of Queensland and the University of New South Wales between 2012 and 2015, using many variations of the design. Details of the first of these experiments are in Murray et. al. (2017).

21 Such as in the case of Glencore, which has been reported to have massively reduced its Australian tax exposure within international loans internal to the company (West, 2014). And the company has form, with the same actions used to dodge taxes on their mining profits in Zambia (Doward, 2011).

22 In economic theory, super-profits are known as economic rents, and they are extra profits available to businesses beyond the 'normal' profits required to justify investment. They are a pure gift from society to the owners of the monopoly rights to mine the country's resources.

23 The group Environmental Justice Australia even has a nice report summarising the 'Six Tricks Coal Mining Companies Play' (Environmental Justice Australia, 2016).

24 Notably, Milner's lobbying firm was co-owned with a former Liberal party staffer David Moore, showing the tight cooperation that apparently oppositional political parties display when there are valuable grey gifts at stake for them and their Mates (Bourke, 2015).

25 The list of names and employment paths was compiled by the office of NSW Greens party MP Jeremy Buckingham (Buckingham, 2015a, 2015b).

26 Total revenues are not discounted or inflated, and are simply the revenues from 1996 to 2015 reported by Ministry of Finance, Statistics Norway, converted to Australian dollars. Data from Ministry of Petroleum and Energy (2017).

27 Economists, sociologists and political scientists have studied this problem for decades, under such labels as 'coalition formation', 'signalling games' and others. We draw on this vast literature here. Academics who have studied criminal gangs and illegal groups, puzzling over how members can be loyal to the rules of the gang, but not to the rules of society, have furthermore helped us home in on the optimal recipe for organising groups of Jameses. One of the present authors, Cameron Murray, extensively surveyed the literature on the issue of signalling and group formation from diverse disciplines including economics, political science, sociology and criminology in his 2016 PhD thesis (Murray, 2016b). We will not be offering further reviews of this extensive literature here.

28 Eddie Obeid was stripped of his Order of Australia after corruption findings by NSW ICAC in 2014 (Wakatama, 2014). Trevor Rowe, whom we mentioned earlier regarding his conflicted roles in Queensland PPP projects, also has an AO. If you start looking, you will

see this surprising pattern, as many researchers have (Spence, 2013). The Order of Australia honour system seems to have been corrupted by the interests of James who simply uses them as another signal of loyalty to his Mates.

29 The Gillard government sought to further reform banking and provided a useful overview of the recent and proposed regulator changes (Australian Government, 2010).

30 Historically speaking, governments also often cheated on money creation. For instance, by investing in their political friends (state-owned enterprises), or by printing money to finance large and wasteful politically motivated projects. Banking has thereby always been a trade-off between the relative degree of criminality of government versus private bankers. One of the myths sustaining James in private banking is that government is less trustworthy than he is.

31 In these simulations, the actual mortgage interest rate is 6 per cent, the potential mortgage interest rate is 5 per cent, and repayments are nominally fixed at $8000 each year, with a 2 per cent inflation rate.

32 The location rules for pharmacies are in Schedule 1 of the National Health (Australian Community Pharmacy Authority Rules) Determination 2018 (PB 65 of 2018).

33 One of the first to monitor this growth was Timothy Devinney, who calculated that the average Australian vice-chancellor made more than twice as much as comparable vice-chancellors in the United States or Europe in 2012. When adjusting for prestige, the difference was closer to triple (Devinney, 2013; Frijters, 2013). More recent analysis shows that the trend has continued to hit the $1 million per year mark (Rowlands and Boden, 2020).

34 Note that we are not counting here the money universities make off foreign students. We cannot count that as either a loss or a gain from the perspective of our typical Australian Sam, as it represents money coming into the country. It may be wastage from the point of view of the countries and families they come from (China, Malaysia, India, Vietnam, etc.), but not from an Australian point of view!

35 The absolute failure of private vocational education training policy should attest to the problems with deregulation under the guise of

competition in a sector such as education, where the nature of the product means that effective competition is impossible.

36 The Hawke reforms of the late 1980s and early 1990s opened up competition in many industries and removed a lot of the subsidies enjoyed by the Jameses of that era. Whilst we are not experts at what preceded that reform era, it seems to us that there were many inefficiencies in the Australian economic system then, but the benefits of those inefficiencies were far more spread out than they are now, which is why inequality reached its low point in the 1970s. If you like, we have gone from a situation where the majority of the population had a proportion of James's winnings to where the Jameses have managed to cut out the share going to regular workers.

37 In the public sector alone, over 230 senior employees in the Australian government currently earn more than the prime minister.

38 In the Netherlands this is controlled by the *Public and Semi-public Sector Senior Officials (Standard Remuneration) Act*. The maximum salary for senior officials in 2015 was €178,000.

39 A more detailed sketch of this plan can be found at the *Club Troppo* website (Frijters, 2021) and in Frijters, Foster and Baker (2021).

40 Indeed, New South Wales has privatised its land title office which is the database that records all property ownership in the state, the accuracy of which is guaranteed by the state (Patty, 2016). The federal government has put forward the idea of privatising ASIC, which is the equivalent database of corporate ownership. These actions are not only a gift to James in terms of selling the government assets, but a gift in adding an additional barrier from outside scrutiny. Michael West, one of the few journalists to use currently transparent data on ownership to call out the Game, extensively critiqued this proposal (West, 2016). The plan was abandoned in December 2016, though we expect the idea to emerge again in the future.

41 We highly recommend the comic 'Can anyone remember the last time they saw the fair go? Maybe we just imagined it?', by First Dog on Moon (Marlton, 2016).